morimoto

morimoto

The New Art of Japanese Cooking

Masaharu Morimoto

Photography by Quentin Bacon

Contents

London, New York, Melbourne,
Munich, and Delhi

Senior Editor Anja Schmidt
Creative Direction & Art Director Dirk Kaufman
Managing Art Editor Michelle Baxter
DTP Coordinator Kathy Farias
Production Manager Ivor Parker
Executive Managing Editor Sharon Lucas

Editor-at-Large Susan Wyler
Introduction, Features, and Glossary Text JJ Goode
Design & Art Direction Gary Tooth / Empire Design Studio
Photography Quentin Bacon

First American Edition, 2007
Published in the United States by
DK Publishing
375 Hudson Street
New York, New York 10014

07 08 09 10 11   10 9 8 7 6 5 4 3 2 1
MD372—September 2007

A catalog record for this book is available from
the Library of Congress.
ISBN 978-0-7566-3123-9

DK books are available at special discounts when
purchased in bulk for sales promotions, premiums,
fund-raising, or educational use. For details, contact:
DK Publishing Special Markets, 375 Hudson Street,
New York, New York 10014 or SpecialSales@dk.com.

Color reproduction by Colourscan, Singapore
Printed in China by Toppan Printing Co., (Shenzen) Ltd.

Discover more at www.dk.com

Introduction

After dinner at one of Morimoto's restaurants, diners often say to him, "We love what we've eaten, but it was not Japanese food." His response, "Why isn't it Japanese, and why must it be?" The very notion of authenticity stands on shaky ground, too fluid to be useful as a way to characterize cuisine. Things change, cultures meld and shift, foods travel across oceans. Many of the ingredients so closely associated with particular cuisines, like chile peppers for Thai and tomatoes for Italian, were themselves at one time imports, centuries ago. In Japanese cuisine as well, many emblematic foods have a foreign pedigree. Soy sauce, sake, tofu, and ramen all came from China. Many believe that tempura-style fried foods were brought to Japan by the Portuguese. Over the centuries, the Japanese incorporated these foreign foods into their diets, cultural and culinary preferences prodding and tugging at them until they took on new forms. Now Japanese soy sauce is distinct from the Chinese version; the two countries adore tofu, but the ways in which each prepares it differ greatly.

Cuisine, according to Masaharu Morimoto, is specific to time and place. Tastes, cooking methods, and technology change over time—what was once impossible is now quotidian, what used to delight is now unappealing—and diners and ingredients differ depending on where they're from. So it follows that there is not just one way to make, say, sushi; instead, says Morimoto, there is Tokyo sushi, Osaka sushi, London sushi, and New York sushi. Morimoto likes to say he cooks 21st-century food. His customers are cosmopolitan; high-tech shipping allows him access to nearly any ingredient, including the pristine seafood, aged soy sauce, and special *nori*, or sea kelp, he buys from Japan. A chef's location no longer determines his larder, and Morimoto uses this modern access to create new enduring combinations, adding oysters, sea urchin, and foie gras to classic trinities like tomato, mozzarella, and basil. He gears his flavors to the new-world palate: In traditional Japanese cuisine, the quality of a chef's clear soup is a measure of his skill—the subtle flavors must build with each mouthful, culminating with the final sip that brings everything together. But since Morimoto makes soup for customers who are used to big, bold flavors, he must make sure each mouthful is complete in itself.

Because Morimoto believes that most of his customers will not relate to traditional Japanese rules of presentation and garnish, in his food he prefers to draw on more suitable points of reference for his playfulness. His culinary creations are full of visual puns. Rock shrimp tempura is slicked with a spicy mayonnaise that brings pleasantly to mind the sauce on Buffalo wings. Ruby-red raw tuna resting on a crispy tortilla is a gloriously reimagined version of pizza.

For his Japanese customers, he has created refined riffs on dishes that represent beloved examples of Japanese culinary fusion. For example, he takes *kare-pan* (Curry Pan, see page 72), the bread stuffed with curried beef that's a staple in Japanese bakeries, and makes the texture irresistibly crispy, the meat more succulent, and the flavors more intense. To him, cooking traditionally means making the best meal possible while working under a set of cultural constraints. He respects those chefs who do it—he's just not willing to be limited by it. And his time in the United States—the great cultural and culinary melting pot—taught him that it was not the only way.

Morimoto is over fifty, but he seems 20 years younger, with an easy smile, mischievous rapid-fire giggle, and dark hair pulled back into a ponytail. He is barrel-chested, still built like the baseball player he once planned to be. Just as he has all his life, he plays hard, always choosing the ambitious over the ordinary. This is the only way to be the pioneer Morimoto aims to be. He pairs Indian-inspired crab naan with Italian bagna cauda; matches raw *fugu* (blowfish) with sweet ripe tomatoes and the best buffalo mozzarella; surprises with bright-red beet soufflé; and turns salmon and squid ink into fluffy gnocchi. Why did he to choose to expand his empire to Mumbai? His answer should not surprise those familiar with this Iron Chef: Because nobody else had.

Yet he does not break rules just for effect or flout tradition willy-nilly—the result must be better than convention. If Morimoto reworks sashimi and his customers yearn for the age-old accompaniments of soy sauce and wasabi, then he has failed. But if he can add new textures and depth of flavor or otherwise up the ante to create a dish that's more interesting and satisfying than the original, then he has succeeded. Paradoxically, to cook food that transcends the traditional, the renegade chef must return to tradition, to the techniques and ingredients in which his cuisine is grounded but not bound to. For instance, Morimoto makes *dashi* (stock made from kelp and cured fish) from scratch, something few chefs do in this country, even those who purport to cook straight Japanese food. Where appropriate for the dish, he enjoys using hard-to-find fresh wasabi, grating it on a sharkskin grater to best coax out its flavor. It's not easy to improve on durable successes, but in this battle, he wields the potential of cuisine unbound by the strictures of tradition. He slicks light-as-air rock shrimp tempura with spicy aïoli, and trades octopus for lobster in his version of *takoyaki*, the popular Japanese street snack. He pairs Peking-style roasted duck legs with red miso sauce instead of hoisin and swaps out Chinese pancakes for a luxurious foie gras-laced croissant, which sandwiches tender duck breast.

EATING AS THEATER

Such exciting food requires an equally exhilarating setting, and Morimoto's restaurants oblige. In his Karim Rashid-designed Philadelphia eatery, the room glows and shimmers, the ceiling undulates, and the color of the booths gradually morph from one neon color to another as you eat. In the stunning New York space, designed by Tadao Ando, one of the world's great architects, a dazzling partition comprised of 17,000 water bottles greets you as you enter, sparkling as if it were made of diamonds. The concrete walls and ceiling ripple like giant curtains—an appropriate setting for the high drama on the plate, the theater that Morimoto believes food deserves. Expect it from waiters, who transform soymilk into delicate, wobbly tofu at your table and unveil neat stacks of layered raw fish—Morimoto's special sashimi—that line up beside diminutive squeeze bottles, each filled with a different sauce.

Using theater is just one way that Morimoto helps customers connect with his food. Another is listening to his diners and gauging their desires. This allows him to manage the delicate balance between insisting customers do things his way and letting them do whatever they want. Give the customer too much and you lose who you are and what you've worked for. Don't give them enough and you have an empty restaurant. What works best, he has decided, is doing whatever the customers want but in such a way that never betrays his guiding principle of deliciousness. If they crave ketchup for their crab, he whips up an exceptionally lively seafood cocktail sauce that will satisfy them, sometimes employing fresh wasabi and *yuzu*, a sweet-tart citron fruit. If they insist on spicy mayonnaise on their sushi rolls, he'll make sure it's the best they've ever tasted. This allows customers a measure of comfort and control, making them more willing to trust him when he decides to test their boundaries, to show them something new. For instance, when you sit down at the *omakase* ("chef's choice") bar for a thrilling, multi-course meal, Morimoto will ask if there's anything you don't like. The most common response, he has found, is, "I like everything but sea urchin." So what will the chef serve for the first course? That's right, sea urchin. Yet because this is not your average sea urchin, most customers find a revelation in the sweet, custardlike roe with its tinge of the sea.

His "don't say no" philosophy extends from his rejection of the dogma of tradition for the principles of pleasure—visceral, giddy pleasure. He embraces his culinary inclinations without hesitation. He did not dither when he thought to pair *gyoza* (pan-fried dumplings) with tangy crème fraîche and earthy tomato sauce. He did not ignore inspiration when it revealed to him that tasty *chawanmushi* (Japanese egg custard) would become something divine were it infused with foie gras.

TWO DREAMS

This pursuit of pleasure at all costs was born out of a childhood of deprivation. Morimoto was born in Hiroshima Prefecture in 1955. His father worked hard as an engineer at a printing company. When he came home in the evening, he frequently drank too much, which did not help his short temper. His mother's family had been wealthy but lost everything during World War II. They were poor and tensions in the Morimoto household ran high, his father flying into a nightly rage and often becoming violent toward his wife. The screaming and fighting got the family evicted from one apartment, then another. By the time Morimoto was 13 years old, they had been forced to move ten times.

A resilient child, Morimoto had two dreams, two ways to escape. For one, he wanted to be a baseball player. As he sat glued to the television, watching a young Sadaharu Oh hit home runs for Tokyo's Yomiuri Giants or cheering for his hometown team, the Hiroshima Carp, his parent's fighting was forgotten. He also fantasized about becoming a sushi chef. The only happy times Morimoto remembers spending with his family were the days when his father received his monthly paycheck. They had a ritual: First, they would stop at a *kissaten* (coffeeshop), where his parents would sip coffee while he and his sister dug into a predinner treat: chocolate sundaes. Then, they would head to a sushi bar. To Morimoto, the sushi chefs that served his family were the epitome of cool. Dressed in crisp white jackets, they exuded confidence and control. They moved with speed and precision, turning out morsels of fish and rice that seemed magically to soothe his parents. His father laughing, his mother smiling, Morimoto stuffing himself blithely—sushi represented a night of peace.

By the end of high school, it was clear that his dream of wielding a knife had taken a backseat to that of wielding a bat. He played catcher and batted cleanup for his school team, which was one of the favorites for the national championships that year. Morimoto's big swing and rifle of an arm brought scouts from the pro team the Hiroshima Carp. That's not to say that he never made a mistake. When he found out that his team's first-round playoff game was going to be televised, he replaced his old, beat-up mitt with a brand new one, the precious "made in the USA" mitt that he had treasured but never used. It certainly looked better, but it was not broken in, and in the seventh inning, he dropped a ball, losing his team the game. For someone who hates to lose, this stung badly at the time (and hasn't fully stopped stinging). To make matters worse, his throwing arm had begun to give out, suffering from overuse. Though he knew that this wouldn't completely dash his chances of making it to the big leagues, he knew that it would always prevent him from being a great player. But there was no obstacle to his becoming a great sushi chef, he thought, so that's what he would do. All he had to do was find a job at a restaurant.

LEARNING THE CRAFT

Almost 25 years before Morimoto became an Iron Chef, before he owned four widely acclaimed restaurants and released his own award-winning beers and splendid saké, he washed dishes at Ichiban sushi, a small restaurant in Hiroshima. It was run by Ikuo Oyama, a kind but demanding chef who prepared a wide range of food, including sushi, sashimi, *udon* (fat, slick noodles), and Japanese curry rice. Morimoto soon became an apprentice to Oyama, living in a room above the restaurant and toiling long hours in the kitchen. Morimoto likes to say that his hours began when he opened his eyes at 5 A.M.

and ended when he closed them at 2 A.M. In the morning, Morimoto would accompany Oyama to the fish market, observing vigilantly as he selected seafood and wrangled with vendors. Later in the day, he would learn to make rice and slice fish. In the evening, he would cook, and at night, he would clean. Every October, he was engrossed in the logistics of Oyama's prosperous side business: selling *matsutake*, the sought-after fall mushroom, which grows in the forests of Hiroshima. Purchasing *matsutake* from villagers and helping Oyama determine to what market and at what price to resell them, Morimoto got his first taste of running a business.

Early in his apprenticeship, he resisted giving himself wholly to the restaurant. Some nights, after he had completed his work, he would sneak out to drink with his friends. This was easier said than done, because Oyama lived next to the restaurant and every night locked the doors from the outside. To escape, burly Morimoto had to squeeze through a small window above the kitchen counter. To ensure a silent getaway, he would shift the chef's van into neutral and push it down the street before he started the engine. Morimoto, it seems, was as conscientious in his mischief as he was in his work.

Soon, however, he gave up partying. If he was going to be a chef, he wanted to become the best chef he could be. He toiled at the craft of cooking sushi rice, aiming to perfect the texture and seasoning. He learned to slice fish not just capably but artfully. He developed a wide breadth of experience, even preparing beloved, humble dishes like *hijiki* (seaweed cooked with soy and sugar), *inari zushi* (fried tofu stuffed with sushi rice), and *korokke* (potato croquettes) for the small food market next door owned by Oyama's brother.

Morimoto believes that had he apprenticed at a more refined restaurant, such as a place that served *kaiseki-ryori*, the intricate and obsessively seasonal meals that developed to accompany the formal tea ceremony, he might not have become the same chef he is today; he might have been too

deeply immersed in tradition and the strict rules of Japanese cuisine to ever break free. After nearly seven years, his apprenticeship was over, but instead of life slowing down, it sped up. He married a woman whom he had met when he was in high school and working part-time at a coffee shop. (He and a friend had applied for jobs as servers. Because of the imposing effect of Morimoto's challenging gaze and sun-tanned face, the owner insisted he work in the kitchen, instead.) At 25, he opened his own café in downtown Hiroshima. A far cry from the tony restaurants whose kitchens he now runs, it was a tiny place with a few tables that dealt mainly in delivery to nearby medical offices and a police station. He cooked simple food—soup, rice, pickles, and a rotating roster of main dishes. At night, he labored as a sushi chef in another restaurant, and in what little free time he had left, he delivered newspapers and worked as an insurance agent at Morimoto Agency, a makeshift outfit that he alone operated. Unsure what he wanted from life, he took on this chaotic schedule, because it allowed him to retreat from the questions he knew he'd soon have to answer.

LIVING IN AMERICA

However busy he was, he couldn't keep his mind from wandering, and this wandering typically took it to the United States. By the late 70s, sushi in the United States had taken off, with dedicated restaurants opening at breakneck speed, especially in Los Angeles and New York City. Morimoto wondered whether he should join the action, even going so far as to send away for a California newspaper in order to peruse the classifieds for job openings. He had a choice to make: With the money he had saved from working—having no time to spend any money meant that he had saved quite a bit—he could stay in Japan and buy a house, a BMW, or an *izakaya*, a Japanese pub featuring small plates of homey food that was growing in popularity at the time. Or he could move to America and toward a life of uncertainty. After much deliberation, he and his wife decided that they would spend a year exploring the United States, visiting New York, New Orleans, San Francisco, and Hawaii before heading back to Japan. Instead, they landed in New York on March 5, 1985, and never left. He had found his home.

Converse sneakers, a Yankees' jersey, and a Rolex watch—these were the three very important purchases Morimoto dreamed about making once he reached the United States. He made them during his first year in New York when he lived in the rough-and-tumble East Village of the 1980s. His apartment on East 6th Street was robbed, so he moved to East 5th Street. When it, too, was robbed, he decided to ditch the neighborhood—his reason, he likes to say, was to protect his new watch. So two years after he arrived, he bought the apartment in which he lives today, even after his rise to fame.

Even the semblance of celebrity was still almost ten years away. Once in the United States, he picked up more or less where he had left off in Japan, working afternoons at one sushi restaurant and nights at another. Yet he had begun to make choices with an eye toward the future. Because he realized restaurants in different areas of the city drew different customers, he made it a point to work at both an uptown and a downtown restaurant. He paid close attention to American preferences, sensing that there must be a way of injecting excitement into what he was serving but not yet knowing what that way should be. After six years of being underpaid and overworked, he began the search for new opportunities.

One day Morimoto saw a job listing in a newspaper for sushi chef at the Sony Club, an exclusive dining room that catered to Sony's executives and talent. It was run by Barry Wine, a pioneering restaurateur, formerly chef/owner of The Quilted Giraffe, a restaurant that was pivotal in introducing "nouvelle cuisine" to the New York culinary scene. Morimoto understood that though he might be good enough to handle the position, he would not likely get it. His resumé, filled with jobs at no-name restaurants in New York and Japan, belied his skill, and in a city that prizes the four-star pedigree, mere talent is not always enough. Nevertheless, he applied. When he didn't get a response from the manager, he called to follow-up. When he still didn't get a response, he almost gave up. As it happened, the manager was planning a party and was short a sushi chef, so in a pinch, sight unseen, he called Morimoto. As soon as he received the call, Morimoto knew he would get the job. And, indeed, the party went well—very well—with Morimoto quickly and deftly producing sushi and sashimi for the hordes of big shots. And when the night was over, he was offered the job.

Morimoto enjoyed working at the Sony Club. He liked riding the elevator with the exquisitely suited executives, stepping off onto the penthouse floor to prepare food for other important people. Morimoto presided over the five-seat sushi bar, tucked away in a small room. The sushi bar catered to Sony's clients and executives and some of their record label superstars. Unlike at most sushi bars in the United States, no glass case separated Morimoto from his customers—they could watch him in action. At first, this made him nervous, but he quickly grew to enjoy the feeling of being "on stage," as it were.

For almost a year, all was well, until a party changed everything. A manager had asked for appetizers and finger food for the guests, but Morimoto misunderstood and enthusiastically prepared as assortment of fabulous "small dish" main courses in no time, instead. To paraphrase, with the expletives omitted, the boss screamed, "This is not a Japanese restaurant!" Morimoto realized that in that position, he would always be in the background, relegated to sushi and appetizers and never allowed to grow and show what he could do. It was time to move on.

NEW FLAVORS

Fortuitously, at the time, Nobuyuki Matsuhisa was planning to open Nobu, the New York sibling of his popular Los Angeles restaurant Matsuhisa. Morimoto decided to look for a position at the new restaurant.

With his first restaurant, chef Matsuhisa had redefined for Americans the concept of Japanese food, serving Peruvian-Japanese fusion dishes based on his travels in South America that incorporated garlic, lime juice, jalapeños, and cilantro to exhilarating effect. The upshot was so wonderfully disorienting that black cod with miso (miso-marinated fish being a long-time home-cooking staple in Japan) came to symbolize a new direction in Japanese cuisine. Nobu restaurant brought that excitement to New York, and in 1994, the restaurant earned two stars from Ruth Reichl, then the *New York Times* restaurant reviewer. Morimoto was there from the beginning, surrounded by new flavors and working under a mandate not to be limited by the strictures of tradition.

Chef Matsuhisa spent much of his time tending to his Los Angeles restaurant, which gave the chefs at Nobu some room to express their own creativity. Morimoto took the lead, preparing wildly imaginative meals for the customers who put themselves in his hands. Within a year, the restaurant garnered a three-star review from Ruth Reichl in the *New York Times.* Morimoto felt at least partly responsible and in his elation, took the liberty of having business cards and a chef's jacket made that referred to him as "executive chef." No one complained; it was clear he had "earned his stripes."

This newfound distinction brought with it new opportunities. When a wealthy Frenchman who owned a summer house in Kenya asked Matsuhisa to come to Africa to cook for him and his family, the chef brought Morimoto along. They flew to Nairobi by private jet and stayed in the Frenchman's lavish compound. Morimoto had planned a week's worth of meals for the family, preparing as much mise-en-scene before the trip as he could and taking it all with him. Matsuhisa stayed for only two days, but by the time he left, all the supplies they brought were used up. What was the future Iron Chef to do? He cooked creatively using only local ingredients to rave reviews (although he ultimately decided against using the camel milk and giraffe leg that he found in the family's freezer).

BECOMING IRON CHEF

Morimoto's big break came during a trip to Japan to see his friends and family. It was the first vacation he had ever taken, and yet he would not leave without cooking one of the most important meals of his career. A Japanese customer at Nobu who adored his food had invited him to cook for a group of her friends in Tokyo. Although he didn't know it then, this group included a judge and a producer from Fuji TV's popular show "Iron Chef." Fortunately, the ever-diligent chef cooked his heart out anyway. Several months later, he got a call from someone from the show. He was sure that he had heard them wrong. Perhaps the man on the phone meant to invite him on as a challenger, he told himself. That would make sense; that he could handle. But the truth frightened him: This man was asking him to be Iron Chef Japanese. For the first time in years, his confidence faltered. Instead of the plucky chef who knew he was skilled enough to work at the Sony Club, who knew he deserved to be executive chef at Nobu, Morimoto suddenly felt provincial and unsure. At first, he declined the offer. But a number of his colleagues started lobbying him, asking him to take the offer because they wanted chefs in their native Japan to recognize the exciting work they were doing in the United States and also to prove how well they cook in a foreign country. (Chefs back home in Japan would often belittle Japanese chefs outside of Japan. Now, various unconventional sushi dishes created by chefs in the United States are adored by people in Japan.) A week later, Morimoto reconsidered and signed on.

He still remembers his first battle. The secret ingredient was *tai* (red snapper), and his opponent was Hirayama Yukio, head chef of Hanya-tei, a respected restaurant in Yokohama. Morimoto felt a strong need to prove himself, to show the Japanese judges what a chef from New York could do. As he battled Chef Yukio, he also had to contend with the fears that the competition brought. Had he made the right decision leaving Japan, eschewing the traditional route for the unconventional one? Was he up to the task of being unfailingly creative again and again, of executing an awe-inspiring procession of dishes in front of the intimidating stare of the camera? Suddenly, he felt as if he were back in Hiroshima during the seventh inning of the game that would decide his team's fate in the playoffs.

Sporting a diamond stud in his ear and swigging from a Coca-Cola bottle as he cooked, Morimoto cut an unusual figure in Kitchen Stadium. His food was equally distinctive. For one of his dishes, Morimoto perched *tai* on top of homemade potato chips, spread with a sauce that combined miso and caviar (an outrageous act in the minds of traditionalists). If you think that took guts, he also served the fish on a bagel. The judges were taken aback but impressed. When they handed down their verdict, it was Morimoto's cuisine that reigned supreme. Morimoto flew to Japan every month until the show ended, about a year after he started.

It was near the end of the original "Iron Chef Japan" that Morimoto had his infamous battle with Bobby Flay, the pugnacious American chef who leaped onto his own cutting board when their hour of cooking was over. In the heat of the moment, Morimoto declared that Flay was "not a chef," because stepping on a cutting board, which is a precious tool, is not what a professional chef would do.

This remark caused quite a bit of controversy, which caught the eye of the Food Network in New York. Soon after the original show's demise in Japan, they decided to produce an American version of the show and asked Morimoto to be one of the four Iron Chefs. This time he didn't hesitate in accepting. A rematch was set up between Morimoto and Flay, which generated a huge audience. That's how "Iron Chef America" began.

Yet while his television persona brought him fame, it was Morimoto's food that truly captivated America. Just as his use of bagels and potato chips captivated the Japanese judges, so did his crab brain dip and caviar tempura bemuse and charm the Americans. He's proud to think that he played a role in raising the status of unconventional food and bringing recognition to Japanese chefs working in America, who a decade ago might have been automatically derided as inadequate by chefs in Tokyo and Kyoto.

ON HIS OWN

"Iron Chef" marked Morimoto's transition from restaurant chef to celebrity chef and made him reconsider his potential. In 1999, after five years at Nobu, he left to pursue opening his own restaurant. He hooked up with Stephen Starr, Philadelphia's prolific restaurateur, who wanted to add a new Japanese restaurant to his portfolio; all he needed was the right chef. But Morimoto had already cooked at someone else's restaurant. Now he wanted to showcase his own food. After balking at first, Starr eventually agreed, giving Morimoto free reign on the food and promising him that after they took Philadelphia, they would do the same in New York. In 2001, Morimoto Restaurant opened in downtown Philly to rave reviews. Craig LaBan, the *Philadelphia Inquirer*'s restaurant critic, called it "Philadelphia's most exciting new restaurant" and described the food as "wondrous."

Yet the opening of his New York restaurant five years later represented the culmination of his career, a triumphant culinary return to the city to which he owes so much. In the city's red-hot Meatpacking District, his resplendent restaurant embodies how far he has come from his days as a dishwasher at Ichiban sushi. Success has chased many fine chefs out of the kitchen and into an office, but Morimoto refuses to relinquish his true love: cooking. You shouldn't be surprised, then, to take a seat at the sushi bar, perhaps his favorite place in the entire restaurant, and see Morimoto standing before you. No kitchen door separates you, so you can watch as he makes magic with fish and rice. For customers, sitting here provides an opportunity to see a master at work. For the chef, working this close to his customers lets him see the blissful grin that follows every bite.

—JJ Goode

Sashimi and Sushi

Fish

The Japanese have developed detailed notions of freshness and seasonality for fish that far exceed most other cultures. For one, Japan is an island nation that has long relied on fish for sustenance. Japan is also one of only a few countries that have historically consumed raw fish. To make my cut, fish must not only be stored correctly right after it has been caught, but it must also be killed properly. Ending a fish's life quickly and painlessly prevents it from struggling, which can harm the quality of the flesh.

Not everyone shares my idea of freshness. Once, I was talking to a fisherman about his salmon. "My fish is fresh," he told me, explaining that he had just then returned to shore. I asked how long he had been out, and his response told me all I needed to know: "Two weeks." That just wasn't good enough for me. I need fish that's been caught days ago, not weeks.

Before the days of modern refrigeration technology, diners could eat only local fish, which had a short distance to travel to their plates. Now I can get astonishingly fresh fish shipped to me from almost anywhere in the world, and I do get much of my fish from Tsukiji, Tokyo's famous fish market. It's not that I don't admire much of the fish from the United States' coasts, particularly the Pacific Northwest, but I naturally prefer ingredients from Japan, because my cooking career as a sushi chef started with Japanese fish, and that is what I am accustomed to.

For novice sushi eaters, it is often the color of each piece that distinguishes one from the other. It's how they learn to tell each fish apart. There's deep red tuna next to deep orange salmon. There's yellowtail, off-white with a rosy hue, beside translucent fluke, a faint dot of green wasabi showing through from below. The more you eat sushi, the more you appreciate the subtle variations in flavor and texture. But with just a little experience, even fish that once seemed similar become distinct. If you haven't yet experienced this revelation, it will come as a happy surprise, as if your palate has awakened after a lifetime of slumber. And your pleasure will only increase as more fish reveal themselves to you. This is why I love serving my more experienced customers the best fish of the season, especially ones they haven't tried before—it's always exciting to discover the taste of a new fish. But I make sure that all the seafood I stock is seasonal and at its peak quality and freshness, so that even fish with which my customers are familiar will be revelatory upon tasting.

Fish of the same type can diverge in texture and flavor. Because they have spent their lives far apart, eating different food and living in varying climates, sea urchin, for example, from the state of Maine, Japan, and Russia all taste slightly different. Even cuts from the same fish can vary, depending on what part of the fish they come from. To illustrate this, let's take a look at one of my favorite fish: the tuna.

There are several kinds of tuna—skipjack, yellowfin, albacore—but bluefin is the best. Large bluefin can weigh over a thousand pounds. They are powerful, able to swim more than 50 miles per hour,

accelerating to that speed in just three seconds. If that description makes tuna sound more like a car than a fish, you might be onto something—I've purchased whole tunas that cost as much as a BMW. The top part of its body is made of lean, red meat called *akami*. It is delicious, though by no means as sought after as its pale-pink belly meat *(toro)*, striated with white fat. Of this, the fattiest (and most expensive) is the *otoro*, the meat over the belly. During the Edo Period, when *nigiri sushi* was invented, no one wanted to eat tuna, because refrigeration technology wasn't able to keep this relatively warm-blooded fish fresh enough. Now that technology has improved, tuna reigns as the king of sushi fish.

Most consumers now know that not all the fish served in Japanese restaurants is raw. But many don't realize that not all fish served as sushi is raw either. To best exhibit the myriad flavors and textures that the oceans of fish provide, I vary the way I treat each one. I leave some completely raw, though I even slice those differently depending on the fattiness and texture. I lightly cure others, such as *kohada* (shad) and *saba* (mackerel), in a mixture of vinegar and salt that makes their flesh slightly firmer and heightens their flavor.

I completely cook some shrimp and eel, among other fish. I thread a skewer through the shrimp—so they don't curl during cooking and can lie flat on the fingers of rice—and dunk them briefly into boiling water. One of the most delicate curing techniques involves lightly salting thinly sliced fish, splashing it with sake, and laying it between sheets of *kombu* (kelp), so that the natural monosodium glutamate in the seaweed—the same kind that's in mushrooms—heightens the flavor of the fish subtly.

Most restaurants don't make the effort to cure and cook seafood themselves, but to me, it goes without saying. After all, the quality of my fish is the highest expression of my skill and judgment as a chef. Several of my variations of preparing and presenting fish follow in this chapter.

Assorted Fish

1. *Unagi shirayaki* (broiled eel)
2. *Madai* (Japanese red snapper)
3. *Kinmedai*
4. *Ike hirame* (fresh fluke)
5. *Ni dako* (cooked octopus)
6. *Mizu dako* (fresh octopus)
7. *Kurumaebi* (prawn)
8. *Ni hamaguri* (cooked clam)
9. *Aori ika* (squid)
10. *Kohada* (shad)
11. *Kisu kobujime*
12. *Sanma* (pike)
13. *Shimaaji*
14. *Maguro akami* (tuna)
15. *Otoro* (fatty tuna)

16. *Chutoro* (medium fatty tuna)
17. *Sayori* (needlefish)
18. *Maaji*
19. King salmon
20. *Shimesaba* (marinated mackerel)
21. Sweet omelet
22. *Uni* (sea urchin)
23. *Shiraebi* (white shrimp)
24. *Sujiko* (salmon roe)
25. *Miru gai* (giant clam)
26. *Hamachi* (yellowtail)
27. *Kampachi* (baby yellowtail)
28. *Ni anago* (cooked sea eel)
29. *Mushi awabi* (steamed abalone)
30. Egg Castella

Slicing fish

After learning how to choose and clean fish, the first thing a professional sushi chef must learn is to slice fish expertly. As I always say, "You need a sharp knife and a sharp arm so that the fibers are cut cleanly, not mashed." Shown here are tuna (*maguro*) and snapper (*tai*) being cut in three basic ways. Pages 22 and 23 show three other variations with squid , needlefish (*sayori*), and horse mackerel (*aji*).

Hirazukuri

The knife cuts straight down to form small slabs of fish. Shown here are *maguro*, or tuna, **(photos 01–03)** and *tai*, or red snapper **(photo 04)**.

Sogi giri

A long knife, held on an angle, is pulled neatly from the base to the tip to cut the fish into slices **(photo 01)**. The tuna slices can be folded into loose cylinders **(photo 02)**, or formed into a rosette **(photos 03–06)**.

Usuzukuri

Paper-thin slices are cut on an angle, shown here with *hirame*, or fluke. First the fin is cut off **(photo 01)**. Then the flesh is carefully separated from the skin **(photo 02)** before it is meticulously sliced **(photos 03 and 04)**. The finished sashimi is arranged on a plate **(photos 05 and 06)**.

Sashimi and Sushi

21

Kanokozukuri

An opened-up squid is cut into a rough rectangle **(photo 01)**. At this point, the squid can be cut several ways, including into thin strips. To make *kanokozukuri*, the strip is laid down outer side up. With the knife held at an angle, the top is scored in one direction **(photo 02)**. Then the piece is rotated 90° and scored again. Note how close together the cuts are made and how adept the chef must be to make these evenly. The opened-up squid body is dipped in very hot water, then in ice water. This tenderizes it. Because the scoring opens up the top, creating a greater surface area, the squid curls after dipping **(photo 03)**. *Kanokozukuri* can be served as a single roll about 1 1/2 inches (4 cm) long or cut into pieces 1/2- to 3/4-inch (2 cm) wide **(photos 04 and 05)**.

◄ Cutting Needlefish

Because of its translucent white flesh and distinctive silvery black stripe, *sayori*, or young needlefish, lends itself to a variety of cuts, several of which are shown here. The fish is trimmed **(photo 01, opposite page)**. The line of skin that runs down the center of the fillet is peeled off **(photos 02 and 03)**. The fish is thinly sliced lengthwise **(photo 04)** and each slice is rolled with one piece of salmon roe in a fold called *warabi*, which is reminiscent of a Japanese mountain vegetable **(photo 05)**. Or it may be thinly sliced crosswise, leaving one edge attached and folded around and under to form a sea chrysanthemum **(photo 06)**, shown filled with finely diced *kimioboro* (egg yolk).

Cross-Hatching Sashimi

To enhance flavor and texture, sometimes other fish, such as *aji*, or horse mackerel, shown here, are cut in a similar fashion to the squid on the opposite page. The skin is removed from the fish **(photos 01–04)**. Then the skin side of the fillet is scored in both directions **(photo 05)**, which reveals the beautiful variation of colors. To serve as sashimi, the fillet is then cut into slices **(photos 06 and 07)**.

Tuna Pizza with Anchovy Aioli

Makes 4 servings

Typical of my combining traditions, this Tuna Pizza is one of my most popular recipes. An instant pizza base is created from a grilled flour tortilla, then topped with tuna sashimi and a sprinkling of colorful vegetables and olives. A tangy Anchovy Aioli is used for garnish and extra eye appeal.

4 flour tortillas, about 7 inches (18 cm) in diameter

2 tablespoons extra virgin olive oil

½ cup barbecued eel sauce (available in Asian specialty stores)

10 ounces (275 g) sushi-grade tuna, thinly sliced

2 fresh jalapeño peppers, seeded and thinly sliced

½ cup thinly sliced red onion

½ cup halved cherry tomatoes

⅓ cup pitted Kalamata olives

Anchovy Aioli

Baby cilantro or sprouts, for garnish

....

ANCHOVY AIOLI
Makes about 1 cup

2 egg yolks

1 tablespoon white wine vinegar

1 tablespoon fresh lemon juice

2 teaspoons anchovy paste

¼ teaspoon soy sauce

¼ cup extra virgin olive oil

½ cup vegetable oil

Salt and freshly ground black pepper

1. Prepare a medium fire in a barbecue grill or set a cast-iron grill pan over medium heat. Brush each tortilla lightly on both sides with olive oil. Brush 2 tablespoons of the barbecued eel sauce over one side of each tortilla.

2. Grill for 1 to 2 minutes, flipping constantly, until crisp. Rotate 90° and grill for 1 to 2 minutes, until crisscross marks appear and the tortillas are fairly crisp. Turn the tortillas over and grill until the second side is crisp, 1 to 2 minutes **(photo 01)**. Transfer to a wire rack to cool.

3. Arrange the tuna slices over the tortillas. Scatter the jalapeño peppers, red onion, cherry tomatoes, and olives over the tortilla. Drizzle the Anchovy Aioli decoratively over the pizza. Garnish with the cilantro or sprouts **(photos 02–05)**.

Anchovy Aioli

While this intensely flavored mayonnaise is used as a decorative sauce on the tuna pizza, it's an excellent accompaniment to steamed or grilled fish and makes a fabulous potato salad. Stored in a tightly covered container, the sauce will keep well in the refrigerator for up to 5 days. **Note: the word "aioli" is used as a conceit here; there is no garlic in the recipe.**

1. In a food processor, combine the egg yolks, vinegar, lemon juice, anchovy paste, and soy sauce. Blend well.

2. With the machine on, very slowly add the olive oil and vegetable oil in a slow, thin stream, processing until the mayonnaise is emulsified and thick. Season with salt and pepper to taste.

Curing Fish

Everyone knows that sushi chefs must be expert at slicing fish, but few realize that a great deal more preparation goes into preparing extraordinary sushi and sashimi than just knife skills. Depending upon the seafood, the season, and the occasion, there are many techniques an accomplished chef must know in order to bring out the best in flavor and texture. These include curing, brining, and simmering ingredients, sometimes in ways that are only noticeable to the most discerning diner. But I know, and when I import the best, hard-to-find seasonal fish from Japan, I want to make sure they get the very best treatment.

Curing with Kelp

Curing with kelp is a traditional way of curing fish fillets or slices ever so slightly between large sheets of *kombu*, or kelp. It takes advantage that this seaweed is naturally very high in monosodium glutamate, a chemical that stimulates the taste buds through the central nervous system, heightening flavor. (Don't worry, by the way, about the use of MSG here. In such a natural form, the amounts absorbed are very small, unlike when it's used as an additive.)

First I choose two prime lengths of top-quality *kombu* and wipe them down on one side with a little sake or rice vinegar **(photo 01)**. I lay out very thin slices of fish moistened side down, on one sheet of kelp, making sure all the fish is in contact with the seaweed and there is no overlap **(photos 02 and 03)**. The sashimi is seasoned lightly with sea salt. (An expert chef will taste the *kombu* to see how much salt is needed.) The second piece of *kombu* is laid on top, sake side down, making contact with the fish **(photo 04)**. The sheets are gently pressed together and the fish is left to "cure" for about 1 hour. The natural MSG in the seaweed seeps into the fish. Whoever eats the sashimi may not know it has been treated, but it will be the most delicious piece of fish they have ever tasted.

Paper and Salt Sashimi

Kamijio is another very subtle way of curing any sashimi, or in this case, very thinly sliced raw octopus. The octopus slices are arranged on a flat plate or tray **(photo 01)**. *Junmai* sake is sprinkled over a sheet of dry rice paper **(photo 02)**, which is then placed over the octopus. I use a traditional Japanese buckwheat mill to grind sea salt to a fine powder **(photo 03)**, which is sprinkled evenly over the top sheet of paper **(photo 04)**; how much you add is up to each chef. Through osmosis, the salt is drawn down through the paper into the octopus, curing it very mildly.

Preparing Salmon Roe

When you eat salmon roe at home, you probably buy it in a jar or tin. Many Japanese restaurants do that, too—in bulk, of course. But I prepare my salmon roe fresh in my own restaurant kitchen, the traditional way they do it on the island of Hokkaido. This way I can control the quality.

I begin with the whole sack of roe from a king salmon. First I carefully peel off the filmy membrane to reveal the eggs clustered underneath **(photo 01)**. Very gently, in a large bowl of hot water, the egg sack is broken apart by hand, like a bunch of grapes **(photo 02)**. Next, I swish the salmon roe around by hand— again, very gently—in the bowl of salted water to enhance the color **(photo 03)** and drain it **(photo 04)**. This is repeated until the water is absolutely clear **(photo 05)**.

I transfer the salmon eggs to a large bowl and ladle a mixture of mirin, sake, soy sauce, and *yuzu* zest over the roe **(photo 06)**. After carefully combining the two, the salmon roe is allowed to marinate for about 3 hours before being drained again.

Curing Fish

Another traditional way of curing fish is with vinegar. *Kohada* is a small fish that has a very special flavor. Like most dark fish, the flavor of *kohada* benefits from a salt and vinegar cure.

   First the head and tail fin are removed, the fish is gutted, and it is rinsed and drained well **(photos 01–03)**. The fish is cut open at the center and the bone is carefully removed, leaving the two fillets attached by skin **(photo 04)**. The fish fillets are arranged on a shallow woven basket, so the liquid can drain, and they are lightly salted on both sides **(photos 05 and 06)**. After curing for 12 minutes, the fillets are rinsed and soaked in a bowl of rice vinegar with the juice of *sudachi* for another 12 minutes to remove excess salt **(photo 07)**. The fillets are arranged skin side up on a clean basket and allowed to drain **(photo 08)**. They should be kept in a container in the refrigerator overnight. For immediate use, cure for a longer period of time.

29

Preparing Clams

Here I introduce a technique we use to make sure the clams you eat at my restaurant are tender and succulent. Their flavor is enhanced through the broth in which they marinate.

First shuck **(photo 01)** and open Japanese cherrystone clams **(photo 02)**, called *hamaguri*. String the pieces on pairs of bamboo skewers **(photo 03)**. Rinse the clams under cold running water to remove any sand **(photo 04)**. Then slide the clams off the skewers into a pot with enough water to cover. Bring the water barely to a boil and cook the clams just until they give up their juices **(photo 05)**. Immediately thereafter, transfer the clams to a bowl of ice and water to stop the cooking **(photo 06)**.

Meanwhile, add a mixture of 1/4 cup each of soy sauce and sugar, and 2 tablespoons each of mirin and sake, to the clam broth **(photo 07)**. Drain the clams, then marinate them for at least 2 hours in the flavored broth **(photo 08)**.

Preparing Octopus

Fresh octopus is a Japanese delicacy. You may wonder how we manage to turn this tough, rubbery mollusk into tender sashimi. It's not easy and, as the name of this sort of preparation—*nimono*—indicates, it involves simmering.

Octopus is covered by a coating of what can only be called slime. The first step in making it edible involves kneading the octopus by hand in a large bowl with a lot of coarse salt to rub off this outer coating **(photo 01)**. After cutting off the body and rinsing off the salt, score the top of the tentacles **(photo 02)** so the arms lie flat. On a wooden board, beat the octopus to tenderize it; a large *daikon* is traditionally used for this purpose because of its tenderizing qualities **(photo 03)**. Then separate the tentacles and dip them a few times into a pot of simmering dashi to heat them gradually **(photos 04 and 05)**. Lower the octopus into the dashi, adding more dashi to the pot if needed **(photo 06)**, and simmer gently until tender, about one and a half hours **(photo 07)**.

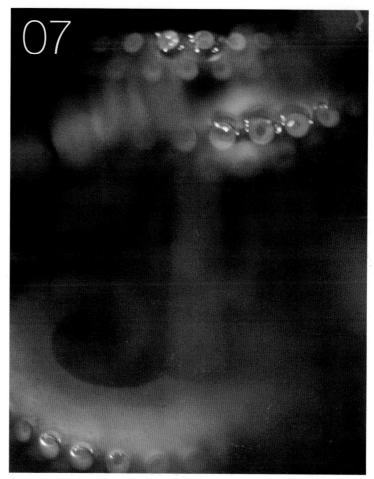

Preparing Vegetables

Katsuramuki

Cutting raw vegetables into paper-thin sheets, a technique called *katsuramuki*, is another technique the expert Japanese chef needs to master. *Daikon* **(photos 01—03)**, cucumber, carrot **(photo 04)**, and sometimes potato are cut this way to use as a sashimi garnish. The accomplished sushi chef does not use a machine, but is able to cut even translucent sheets free-form, with nothing but a knife.

Sasagiri

In ordinary restaurants, plastic copies of bamboo leaves are used for plating. In my restaurant, we use a *sasagiri* knife and techniques on real bamboo leaves **(photo 01)** to improve my chefs' knife skills **(photos 02–04)**. The results are shown in photos 05 and 06. In Japan, there are *sasagiri* competitions.

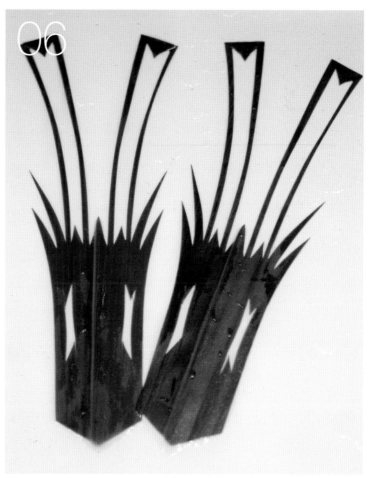

Nori

I can hear it crackle like kindling on fire, as I carefully cup a half sheet of nori in one hand. With the other, I add a layer of rice and a bit of fish. Quickly—for there is no time to spare—I wrap the nori around these ingredients to form a cone-shaped parcel. This is *temaki*, or a hand roll, and it's perhaps the ideal way to enjoy high-quality nori. While this Japanese sea vegetable is referred to as mere "seaweed" in America, this is an unfair moniker. A weed is something you don't want, and I promise you, you do want my nori.

Unlike *nori maki*, the most common sushi, *temaki* is made so quickly that the moisture from the air and rice has no time to leach into the nori, making it soggy. Instead, when you bite into the roll, it crunches under your teeth and melts quickly in your mouth, revealing an oceanic tang, a whiff of the sea. I suggest *temaki* to customers who sit at the sushi bar, because the height of the nori's crispness won't survive a trip to the table. It is my gift to those who choose to sit directly in front of me, who put themselves in my hands.

Officially, nori is a red algae, which might sound strange given that most of us know nori as the strip of greenish black outside of our sushi rolls. In fact, nori is a reddish-brown color when fishermen harvest it from Ariake, Tokyo, and Seto-uchi bays. As with cheese or wine, the companies that make sheets of nori from the harvested product vary from large operations that mass-produce nori to small, family-run businesses whose care is evident in their product. Either way, the process is similar: Nori is made into a mash and spread thinly—think cream cheese on a bagel—onto a flat surface. Then it is dried, peeled off, and cut into 8 x 7 1/2 inch (20 x 19 cm) sheets. Finally, most nori is toasted, which brings out its flavor and turns it that familiar dark green. Before it's sold, nori is sorted into many grades, which vary widely in price. The quality, and hence price, of the nori varies according to weather, location, and sea conditions of the place where it is harvested. It's worth buying the best you can find.

This is not to say that you can't enjoy nori in other ways. Nori usage is by no means restricted to sushi. In Japan, nori shows up nearly everywhere you look: wrapped around *onigiri*, fist-sized balls of rice stuffed with *tarako* (cod roe) or *ume* (the savory pickled Japanese apricot), among other treats; shredded and sprinkled on top of *soba* noodles; or accompanying a traditional Japanese breakfast, where pieces of nori appear in a pile beside a bowl of white rice and small dish of soy sauce. You use your chopsticks to grab a small piece of nori, dip one side of it in the soy sauce, and use it to nab some rice.

Outside of Japan, nori makes its most frequent appearance in *nori maki*, which is rolled in a bamboo mat and sliced in pieces. Its flavor provides a deliciously briny, slightly smoky accent to the rice and fish or vegetable, even if it does not sport the supreme crispness of a hand roll. If along with *nigiri sushi* (morsels of fish on top of fingers of rice), you see hand rolls on your plate, you may want to eat them quickly so you catch the nori when it's still slightly crisp. This is why I prefer not to serve inside-out rolls—that is, rolls whose outermost layer is rice, not nori. In these, the nori is hidden, its subtle flavor obscured. However, when a customer requests an inside-out roll, I am happy to give them what they want, still making it with the highest quality nori.

You'll find nori in some shape or form in the cupboards of most Japanese people, so it should come as no surprise that the Japanese eat about 10 billion sheets per year. In the United States, as you might imagine, that number is far less, though it's in the hundreds of millions and growing quickly. Nori happens to be packed with vitamins A and B, as well as calcium and iron. That's why it used to be available not only in Asian specialty stores, but in health food stores. Now you can find it in many supermarkets throughout the United States.

The nori I use, which suits my sushi best, comes from Japan, where it has been cultivated for centuries. I won't reveal how much it costs—that wouldn't be gentlemanly, would it?—but I will tell you about it. The best Japanese nori is harvested by fishermen in Ariake Bay, off the coast of Kyushu. Of this, I buy *shin nori*, or nori from the first harvest, which has the cleanest flavor and the most delicate texture.

Assorted Sashimi

1. *Shimaaji*
2. Scallop
3. *Aoyagi* (orange clam)
4. *Madai* (Japanese red snapper)
5. *Kurumaebi* (prawn)
6. *Madai* (Japanese red snapper)
7. *Maguro akami* (tuna)
8. *Spiny lobster head*
9. *Tokobushi* (baby abalone)
10. *Maguro* (tuna)
11. *Kurumaebi* (prawn)
12. *Salmon wrapped with cucumber*

13. *Maguro* (tuna)
14. *Otoro* (fatty tuna)
15. *Uni* (sea urchin)
16. *Ika mentaiko* (squid with cod roe)
17. *Sayori* (needlefish)
18. *Maguro akami* (tuna)
19. Fresh wasabi
20. *Nidako* (cooked octopus)
21. *Shimesaba*
    (cured mackerel)

Mizu Gai Sashimi

This is a very special summertime dish and, as you can see at left, it is a delight to the eye as well as to the taste buds. An assortment of firm fish, shellfish, and colorful vegetables are arranged in a container. Ice-cold sparkling wine is poured over all; if it's a *mizu gai* that I am eating, you can be sure I will use Dom Perignon—but, seriously, any dry sparkling white wine serves well. To eat, pick up a delicacy from the dish, then dip it in aged soy sauce or *irizake*, a special sauce I make from sake and green plum. At the end, the wine can be ladled into small bowls and drunk.

Bocconcini de Buffalo Sashimi

Here I go with the Italian again. I cannot resist. Why should we be restricted to a palette of flavors from only one cuisine, when so many foods go together beautifully? The creamy mild flavor and soft texture of fresh mozzarella is a perfect foil for sashimi. In Italy, it is traditionally paired with prosciutto. So I pair little balls of fresh water buffalo mozzarella, called *bocconcini*, with an assortment of raw fish and a slice of prosciutto. The fish here includes sea scallop, king salmon, and baby octopus. With a nod to the Italian caprese salad, a few cherry or grape tomatoes are added, along with dill, shiso bud, and *benitade* as a garnish. A drizzle of olive oil, some sea salt, and a few dabs of aged soy sauce finish off the plate.

How to Eat Sushi

To the sushi novice, nothing seems simpler than sushi—
a morsel of fish, often uncooked, on top of a fat finger of rice.
The sushi chef forms *nigiri sushi* so quickly, so effortlessly
that you'd be forgiven for assuming that there is not much
to the craft. But these are deliberate gestures, developed over
years of practice. And preparing rice and fish that will make
my customers swoon is anything but simple.

I've spent many years honing my technique for
making vinegared rice, or *sumeshi*. I buy the best rice, mill
it myself, and cook it so that each grain is perfect. I spread
the rice in a wood basin called a *hangiri*, so that when I add
a painstakingly proportioned mixture of high-quality rice
vinegar, salt, and sugar, it will distribute evenly, coating each
grain with a cloak of sweet acidity. I form each finger of rice
with my hands so that it's packed neither too densely nor too
loosely, so it bursts apart in your mouth. I've also spent years
building relationships with fish distributors and working on
my technique for preparing fish. I learned how to skillfully
cut tuna in order to make beautiful, jewel-like pieces of sushi,
how to score squid so it's just barely chewy, and how to
lightly cure certain fish, like *kohada* (shad).

I don't believe strict rules should govern how you
eat every bite of food, yet I do hope customers will appreciate
the efforts I've taken to create balanced, delicious sushi by
considering the following advice:

Don't dunk your sushi rice-first into soy sauce. This spoils
the texture of the rice that I've worked so hard to
create and overwhelms the delicately seasoned rice.
At my sushi bar, I add just the right amount and
type of soy sauce to the fish in each piece of sushi,
so there's no need to add more. This small blast of
heady saltiness snaps your palate to attention, getting
it ready for the subtle flavors of the fish and rice.
If you must add more, however, please invert your
sushi and let the fish graze the sauce.

And, please, don't mix wasabi into your soy sauce. I've
noticed that many American diners practice an
identical ritual when their sushi arrives. I've watched
them nab a wad of wasabi with their chopsticks and
plunge it into their dish of soy sauce. Ideally, the
sweet bite of the wasabi tucked under the fish and
the rich, salty slick of soy on top should meet each
other in the mouth, not before. This creates an
exciting friction that's lost when they are combined
into a murky sauce. And it's up to the skilled sushi
chef to add the appropriate amount of wasabi for
the strength of the fish.

Eat the pickled ginger between bites of sushi, not with bites of sushi. The pickled ginger *(gari)* that accompanies sushi is especially tasty when it's homemade. Yet it does not belong draped over sushi, where it overshadows the other flavors. Instead, it's meant to be eaten between pieces of sushi—its pleasant astringency and sweet-tart tang rejuvenates your palate, preparing you for the next exciting sensation.

Like all Japanese food, sushi is meant to be experienced with all the senses. You see the vivid red of tuna next to stark white squid and bright orange sea urchin; you smell the soy; you hear the snap of your teeth biting through crisp nori. So why shouldn't you eat each piece of sushi with your hands, to feel the warm, sticky rice and weight of the fish? It is perfectly acceptable, though personally, since I'm usually watching, I prefer the elegance of chopsticks.

Finally, don't nibble my sushi. I've carefully determined the proportions of fish, rice, and wasabi in each piece of sushi to create the perfect mouthful, so I want my customers to eat it in just one bite. Many of my customers are reluctant to do this, and ask whether I can cut each piece in half. I say, "Sure, as long as you put both pieces in your mouth at once!"

Assorted Sushi

1. *Kampyo roll* (cooked squash)
2. *Sayori ikura* (needlefish with salmon roe)
3. *Sayori kimioboro*
4. *Chutoro* (medium fatty tuna)
5. *Maguro akami* (tuna)
6. *Otoro* (fatty tuna)
7. *Kampachi* (baby yellowtail belly)
8. King salmon
9. *Oboro kyuri* roll
10. Egg Castella
11. *Ikura* (salmon roe)
12. *Shikai maki*
13. *Kurumaebi* (prawn)
14. *Ika ajisai* (squid flower)
15. Shrimp tempura roll

16. Spicy tuna roll
17. Shrimp tempura roll
18. *Kinmedai*
19. *Madai* (Japanese red snapper)
20. *Aoyagi* (orange clam)
21. *Engawa menegi* (fluke fin with baby scallion)
22. *Ika* (squid)
23. *Aji* (horse mackerel)
24. *Nihama* (cooked clam)
25. *Unagi shirayaki* (broiled freshwater eel)
26. *Ni anago* (cooked sea eel)
27. *Uni* (sea urchin)
28. *Shimesaba* (cured mackerel)
29. *Mushi awabi* (steamed abalone)

01

02

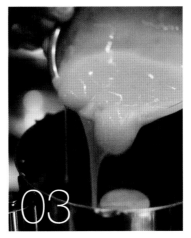

03

04

05

06

07

08

09

Japanese Egg Castella

Makes 12 to 16 servings

¼ cup sake

¾ cup sugar

½ pound (225 g) shrimp, shelled and deveined

16 egg yolks

2 tablespoons milk

2 tablespoons heavy cream

2 tablespoons all-purpose flour

12 egg whites

You'll find this alternative to Japanese Sweet Egg Omelet at only the best sushi restaurants. It has a sweet syrup and puréed shrimp added to the batter, as well as a little flour, milk, and cream. In addition, the eggs are separated and the whites whipped until stiff and folded in, so the effect is quite different. We bake the castella batter in a special rectangular omelet pan. For this recipe, you can use a 9 x 13 inch (22 x 32 cm) baking pan.

1. Preheat the oven to 350°F (180°C). In a small, heavy saucepan, combine the sake and sugar. Bring to a boil, stirring to dissolve the sugar.

2. In a food processor or blender, purée the shrimp (photo 01) for at least 2 minutes, until they form a completely smooth paste (photo 02). Add the egg yolks (photo 03), milk, and heavy cream. Blend well. Gradually beat in the hot syrup in a thin stream (photo 04). Dust the flour over the batter and whisk until well blended (photo 05).

3. In a large mixer bowl, beat the egg whites until stiff peaks form (photo 06). With a large whisk, fold and mix the egg whites into the batter, trying to deflate the mixture as little as possible (photo 07).

4. Turn into an oiled baking pan and bake for 30 minutes, or until the egg castella is puffed and golden brown on top and set through (photos 08 and 09). Test by inserting a skewer and pulling it out clean.

Chirashi Zushi

In Japanese, *chirashi* literally means "scattered." But you won't find me scattering anything; all the sashimi I prepare is carefully arranged. For this dish, I choose an assortment of sashimi and casually, though artfully, arrange it over a bed of sushi rice. Depending upon the season and what is available that day, the topping can vary tremendously. Here we used Japanese sweet egg omelet, sea urchin *(uni)*, lotus root, pickled *myoga*, blanched sugar snap peas, salmon roe *(ikura)*, fatty tuna *(otoro)*, horse mackerel *(aji)*, and needlefish *(sayori)*, among other fish.

Broiled Mackerel Sushi

While this chapter has focused on raw or lightly cured seafood, sometimes sushi is lightly cooked. This is especially true of very oily fish, like eel and mackerel. For the type of sushi shown in this photo, called *oshi zushi*, which is typical in the west of Japan, the cooked rice is pressed into a form and then cut with a knife, rather than being formed into a mound by hand. The fish is cured, placed on the rice, and then broiled. Instead of plain, grated wasabi, it is served with a special scallion-wasabi. Here the sushi is shown with pickeled ginger (*gari*) and *kinome* (see Glossary on page 262). A slash of wok-smoked balsamic vinegar completes the plate.

Sushi Rice

Quality of rice is one of the hallmarks by which you can judge a sushi restaurant. In Japan, every chef who is traditionally trained first learns how to make rice—perfectly. In Asia, almost everyone prepares rice in an electric rice cooker. It is simply the easiest, most energy efficient, and most sensible way to make perfect rice every time. Even in a restaurant, we use huge rice cookers. What is critical, however, is what you do to the rice after it is cooked. Sushi rice has to be subtly flavored, and worked properly as it cools, to obtain the perfect texture for sushi.

After cooking, the short-grain white rice is turned into a large wooden bowl or tub **(photo 01)**. The hot rice is worked with a large wooden spatula **(photo 02)**. Sushi Vinegar is added to season the rice, poured over the spatula to drizzle gently onto the rice **(photo 03)**. The rice is not stirred, but is cut sideways and folded over so that the flavoring is evenly incorporated and the moisture evaporates **(photos 04 and 05)**. You need to keep cutting to break up any lumps of rice **(photo 06)**. The finished, partly cooled rice begins to separate into individual grains as you keep flipping it over, removing each individual grain off

the spatula to avoid their becoming dry **(photos 07 and 08)**. Then the rice is left to set for 5 to 10 minutes before being formed into actual sushi.

NOTE: **You can judge the quality of sushi partly by the temperature of the rice. Freshly made sushi rice will be room temperature, or even slightly warm, not too cold.**

Sushi Vinegar
To use with 10 cups cooked rice.

Of course you can buy seasoned rice vinegar in the supermarket, but it tastes better if you make it yourself at home, and you can adjust the ingredients to your preference. Here is my recipe.

½ cup sake-mash vinegar *(akazu)*, or regular white wine vinegar

½ cup rice vinegar

½ cup sugar

¼ cup salt

1. Combine all the ingredients. Stir to dissolve the sugar. Pour into a covered container. The Sushi Vinegar will keep for at least 2 months refrigerated.

Rice

GREEN IN THE FIELD

WAS POUNDED INTO

RICE CAKE

—MASAOKA SHIKI (1867–1902)

While the herbed rice cake flavored with wild greens conjured up in this haiku appeals to my senses, it particularly moves me because, besides being a great author and literary critic, Shiki is credited with introducing baseball to his hometown in Japan. He loved the game, and his nickname, "Noburu," was a play on the Japanese words for "ball field." As many know, I started out aiming to be a professional baseball player, so it's a particularly appealing poem for this chef.

It is sometimes hard for people to grasp just how important rice is to Japanese culture. Like potatoes to the Irish, it is, first of all, the basis of all sustenance. In early times, this staple was used as a medium for paying taxes. Samurai received their salaries in the form of rice. And much of Japanese cuisine evolved in the perfection of cooking rice. Sushi, remember, refers not to the fish, but to the vinegared rice, and it is by the nuanced characteristics of the rice cake under the fish, as well as the quality and cut of the fish itself, that a great sushi chef is judged.

I am told by many that they could pick out my sushi in a blind tasting. And much of that distinction is owed to the rice. It makes me very glad to hear that, since at the beginning of my career, I spent four years learning how to cook rice before they even let me pick up a knife!

If this rigorous training surprises you, you are in for a treat—that is, if you love Japanese food. By learning to understand rice and to taste it properly, you will raise your level of appreciation of much of Japanese cooking. All my food is a celebration of the senses—visual as well as gustatory—and anyone can enjoy it. But if you really pay attention, you will experience the food at another level.

What makes my rice so special actually goes beyond cooking. You see, in Japan, I would use a blend of two different varieties of rice: *koshi kikari,* which is the very best but is too strong by itself, and *akita komachi* or *sasa nishiki,* to temper the flavor. Unfortunately, I cannot obtain these particular types of rice in the United States, so I've devised my own system: I order the best-quality brown sushi rice available from California, and I polish it myself.

Brown rice, with the outside husk intact, remains fresher much longer than unprotected white rice; that's one reason I begin with the whole grain. Each morning we decide how much rice we will need for the restaurant, and just enough is processed for that day. My special machine lets me decide exactly how far to take the polishing. I always leave a little of the outside for flavor and texture while being careful to preserve the entire *haiga,* or rice germ inside. That's why when you taste my sushi, the rice sticks together yet each kernel has its own integrity.

Beyond sushi, there are many different rice dishes and categories of rice dishes in Japanese cuisine. In this book, you'll find a wide range of appealing rice recipes: from Buri Bop (see page 54) and Sushi Rice Risotto (see page 60) to my play on Chinese congee, Scallop Congee (see page 148). Some have many other ingredients and techniques involved. But always keep in mind that while the rice may seem as if it is just the humble foundation, without the proper base, the rest of the dish will be lacking. And since I know you cannot polish your own rice, I simply recommend you purchase the best quality sushi rice available to you.

CHEF'S NOTE: **Here's an interesting and very traditional trick you can use when cooking rice. Place a piece of Japanese charcoal, bintan, right in the pot with the rice and water. Just like activated charcoal used for filtering, it will remove any impurities from the water and will make your rice taste even better. Just make sure you use genuine bintan and not ordinary charcoal or charcoal briquettes. Bintan can be purchased in some Asian specialty stores.**

Rice, Noodles, Breads, and Soups

Buri Bop

Makes 4 servings

I love the name Buri Bop. It sounds a little like rock and roll, which is what I like my food to do. Actually, *buri* is another Japanese name for yellowtail, or *hamachi*, and *bop* is an allusion to a kind of Korean dish, *biiambap*, cooked in a hot stone bowl. This technique gives the rice base a nice golden crust, and the rest of the food is cooked right on the hot walls of the bowl. For the drama of presentation alone, it is worth searching out these stone bowls at Korean or other Asian markets (see Sources on page 265).

1½ cups short-grain white rice, well rinsed and drained

1 pound (450 g) yellowtail (*hamachi*) or other fatty-flesh, sushi-grade fish, cut very thinly into about 32 slices

¼ cup Garlic-Soy Jus (page 152), plus more for serving

1 tablespoon sesame oil

Sesame Oil-marinated Spinach (recipe follows)

Marinated Royal Fern (recipe follows)

Picked Daikon and Carrot (recipe follows)

4 large egg yolks

Yuzu pepper (*yuzu kosho*, available in Asian specialty stores)

¼ cup finely shredded nori (*kizami nori*)

1. Preheat the oven to 500°F (260°C). Place 4 stone or heatproof earthenware or heavy ceramic bowls in the oven to heat through until searingly hot, 20 to 30 minutes.

2. While the bowls heat, cook the rice in a rice cooker or as follows: Place the rinsed rice in a medium saucepan, add 1½ cups cold water, and cover. Bring to a boil over high heat. Reduce the heat to low and simmer until the rice is tender, about 8 minutes. Remove from the heat and let stand, covered, for 5 to 10 minutes.

3. Mix the *hamachi* with ¼ cup of the Garlic-Soy Jus in a small bowl. Marinate at room temperature for no longer than 30 minutes.

4. Using mitts to handle them, carefully remove the hot bowls from the oven. Working very quickly, brush the interior of each stone bowl with sesame oil. Rinse an 8-ounce (225 g) custard or coffee cup with water. Pack the hot rice into the cup and invert into a hot bowl to unmold. Flatten the rice slightly so it spreads a bit in the bowl—be sure to leave an inch or so of the inner sides of the bowl exposed. Repeat to fill all 4 bowls.

5. Arrange equal amounts of the Sesame Oil-marinated Spinach, Royal Fern, and Pickled Daikon and Carrot around the rice. Carefully slip an egg yolk onto the center of each hot rice mound. Remove the *hamachi* from the marinade and arrange 8 slices over each yolk in a spoke pattern. Top with a pinch yuzu pepper and shredded nori. Drizzle a little of the Garlic-Soy Jus around the side of the bowl.

6. Again using mitts, place each pot on an underliner or on a heatproof plate at the table. Each guest uses chopsticks to "cook" the *hamachi* slices against the sides of the hot bowl. To eat, mix up the rice, toppings, and sauce and retrieve the seared *hamachi* from the sides of the bowl.

continued . . .

Sesame Oil-marinated Spinach

Makes 4 servings

While used here as one of a number of ingredients in Buri Bop, it makes a nice cooked salad on its own.

1¼ pounds (560 g) baby spinach, rinsed

1 tablespoon sesame oil

Sea salt

1 tablespoon sesame seeds

1.   Bring a large pot of water to a boil. Add the spinach and cook until bright green, about 1 minute. Drain and rinse under cold running water. A handful at a time, squeeze out excess water from the spinach.

2.   Transfer the spinach to a bowl. Toss with the sesame oil and salt to taste. Sprinkle the sesame seeds on top. To store, cover and refrigerate for up to 1 day.

Marinated Royal Fern

Makes 4 servings

Royal fern is easily found in packages in the refrigerated section of any Japanese grocery. For more details, see the Glossary on page 262. These small fern shoots have a delicious chewiness that adds textural interest to the Buri Bop.

2 teaspoons sesame oil

2 garlic cloves, grated

8 ounces (225 g) royal fern *(zenmai)* drained, rinsed, and patted dry (about 1½ cups)

2 tablespoons soy sauce

2 tablespoons mirin

2 tablespoons sake

1.   Heat the sesame oil in a medium skillet over medium heat. Add the garlic and cook, stirring often, until fragrant, about 1 minute. Add the royal fern, soy sauce, mirin, and sake. Cook over medium heat, stirring several times, until the liquid has reduced to about 2 tablespoons, about 20 minutes. To store, cover and refrigerate for up to 1 day.

Pickled Daikon and Carrot

Makes about 2 cups

This refreshing pickle needs to marinate overnight, so start at least a day before serving.

12 ounces (350 g) daikon

1 large carrot

2 tablespoons coarse salt

1 cup rice wine vinegar

½ cup sugar

1.   The day before serving, peel the daikon and carrot and trim off the ends. Thickly shred on the julienne disk of a food processor or on a Japanese mandoline. Toss with the salt in a colander and let drain for 1 hour.

2.   Meanwhile, bring 1 cup water, vinegar, and sugar to a boil in a nonreactive medium saucepan, stirring to dissolve the sugar. Remove from the heat and let cool for 1 hour.

3.   Rinse the salt off the daikon and carrots. Add to the vinegar mixture and stir well. Cover and refrigerate overnight. Drain before serving.

Stuffed Lotus Leaves

Makes 6 servings

1¼ cups sticky rice (available at Asian specialty stores)

6 dried lotus leaves or 3 large leaves, cut in half

1½ cup Shanton Broth or Chicken Stock (page 256)

3 tablespoons soy sauce

3 tablespoons oyster sauce

1 tablespoon plus 1 teaspoon sugar

1 teaspoon ground white pepper

Salt

2 tablespoons vegetable oil

1 tablespoon minced scallion

½ teaspoon fresh grated ginger

½ teaspoon minced garlic

4 ounces (100 g) skinless, boneless chicken thigh, diced

4 ounces (100 g) shrimp, shelled and deveined, diced

5 fresh shiitake mushrooms, stemmed and diced

¼ cup water chestnuts, diced

2 tablespoons sake

1 teaspoon salt

Pinch ground white pepper

2 tablespoons cornstarch, dissolved in 2 tablespoons water

1 tablespoon sesame oil

This recipe for *chimaki*, or stuffed lotus leaves, represents my interpretation of a traditional Chinese dish, often part of a dim sum. Savory rice loaded with tasty ingredients is wrapped inside lotus leaves and steamed. The bundle is untied at the table. When you serve, make sure everyone gets some of the treats inside. Because the rice must soak before cooking, be sure to begin this recipe at last 4 hours before you plan to cook the dish.

1. Put the rice in a strainer set over a bowl. Fill the bowl with cold water, swish the strainer around in the bowl to remove the surface starch, then lift the strainer out and discard the water. Repeat this rinsing 3 times or until the water is mostly clear. Put the rice in a bowl and add enough fresh cold water to cover. Let stand for at least 4 and up to 6 hours. Meanwhile, soak the lotus leaves in water until they soften.

2. Drain the rice and steam in a bamboo steamer over a large pot of boiling water for 30 to 40 minutes or in a rice cooker, until the rice is just tender all the way through each grain.

3. Put the steamed rice into a large bowl. Add ½ cup of the Shanton Broth, 1 tablespoon each of the soy sauce and oyster sauce, 1 teaspoon each of the sugar and white pepper, and salt to taste. Mix well to season evenly.

continued . . .

Stuffed Lotus Leaves continued

4. In a medium saucepan, heat the oil with the scallion, ginger, and garlic over medium heat. Add the chicken, shrimp, mushrooms, and water chestnuts and cook, stirring, until the chicken turns white, about 3 minutes. Add the remaining 1 cup stock, 2 tablespoons each soy sauce, oyster sauce, and sake, 1 tablespoon sugar, 1 teaspoon salt, and an additional large pinch of white pepper to the pan. Bring to a boil, reduce the heat to a simmer. Stir in the dissolved cornstarch. Bring to |a boil, stirring until thickened. Add the sesame oil and transfer to a bowl. Let the filling cool.

5. Smooth out a lotus leaf and place about ½ cup of the seasoned rice in the center **(photo 01)**. Spread out to form a rectangle about ½-inch (1 cm) thick, with a raised rim all around **(photo 02)**. Top with 3 tablespoons of the filling **(photo 03)**. Top with another ½ cup of rice and press down firmly on the edges of the cake to seal the filling inside **(photo 04)**. Wrap the lotus leaf around the rice cake **(photos 05 and 06)**. Roll up to form a neat rectangular packet, about 5 x 3 inches (12 x 7 cm) **(photo 07)**. Repeat to make 6 packets in all.

6. Put the stuffed lotus leaves in a bamboo steamer **(photo 08)**. Steam over boiling water seam side down for 10 minutes, until heated through. Serve hot.

08

This recipe offers a quick and delicious way to use leftover rice. Of course, markets sell preseasoned sushi vinegar, but it is easy and much better to make it yourself so you can control the amount of sweetness and tartness.

Sushi Rice Risotto

Makes 4 servings

1½ cups cooked short-grain white rice

2½ tablespoons Sushi Vinegar (page 48)

3 cups Dashi (page 256)

1 teaspoon light-colored soy sauce

2 eggs, beaten

2 teaspoons grated fresh wasabi*

1 tablespoon shredded nori (kizami nori)

3 or 4 sprigs of mitsuba leaves, minced, or chopped scallions or chives, for garnish

1. Reheat the cooked rice in a steamer or microwave.

2. Put the hot rice in a bowl and toss with the Sushi Vinegar. Let cool.

3. Transfer the rice to a medium saucepan and pour the Dashi over it; stir to combine. Bring to a boil, uncovered. Reduce the heat to medium-low and simmer for 3 to 4 minutes.

4. Add the light-colored soy, then pour the eggs right over the rice without stirring. Cook for 10 to 15 seconds, until the eggs are barely set. Remove the pan from the heat.

5. Divide the rice among individual bowls and top each with wasabi, nori, and mitsuba. Serve immediately.

*In this recipe, frozen wasabi paste or paste made from the powder may be substituted if fresh is unavailable.

Za Jan Noodles

Makes 4 servings

1 tablespoon vegetable oil

½ pound (225 g) ground pork

1 tablespoon minced
fresh ginger

1 tablespoon minced garlic

¼ cup julienned bamboo
shoots

1½ cups Shanton Broth
or Chicken Stock (page 256)

¼ cup red miso

¼ cup soy sauce

2 tablespoons sugar

2 tablespoons sake

1 teaspoon cornstarch,
dissolved in ¼ cup cold water

1½ teaspoons
Asian sesame oil

Salt and freshly ground
white pepper

12 ounces (350 g) dried
thin noodles, such as *ramen*
or *lo mein*

½ cucumber, peeled, seeded,
and julienned

1 hard-boiled egg, chopped

1 scallion, thinly sliced

Sprigs of baby cilantro

Mildly seasoned, with a jumble of
Japanese flavors from miso to sake,
these noodles with a savory pork sauce
are easy to prepare for a weeknight
supper, especially if your pantry
is stocked with Japanese ingredients,
which I hope it will be from now on.

1. To make the sauce, heat the oil in a large skillet over
medium-high heat. Add the ginger and garlic and cook,
stirring often, about 2 minutes. Add the ground pork and
cook, breaking up any large pieces with a wooden spoon,
until the liquid evaporates, about 6 minutes. Stir in the
bamboo shoots.

2. Mix the Shanton Broth, red miso, soy sauce, sugar, and
sake in a bowl to dissolve the miso and sugar. Stir into the
skillet and bring to a boil. Add the dissolved cornstarch and
cook until the sauce thickens. Remove from the heat and stir
in the sesame oil. Season with salt and white pepper to taste.
Cover the sauce to keep it warm while you cook the noodles.

3. Bring a large pot of water to a boil over high heat. Add
the noodles and cook until tender, about 4 minutes, or
according to the package instructions. Drain and divide
among 4 bowls.

4. Spoon the sauce over the noodles and top with the
cucumber, chopped egg, scallions, and baby cilantro.
Serve immediately.

Pork Gyoza

with Rustic Tomato Sauce and Bacon-Cream Reduction

Makes 8 servings, about 48 dumplings

You may notice a slight similarity between my sauced pork and cabbage-filled gyoza and Italian meat ravioli. Of course, I enjoy pasta as much as the next person, but I am always compelled to translate what I taste into my own version of Japanese food. Serve these as a first course or with a salad for a light supper or lunch.

3 cups finely shredded Napa cabbage

¼ cup chopped chives, preferably garlic chives

1 tablespoon coarse salt

12 ounces (350 g) fatty ground pork, such as shoulder

½ teaspoon freshly ground black pepper

1 package (10 ounces/275 g) gyoza wrappers, about 50 wrappers

¼ cup vegetable oil

½ recipe Rustic Tomato Sauce (recipe follows)

Bacon-Cream Reduction (recipe follows)

1. To make the dumplings, toss the cabbage and 3 tablespoons of the chives with the salt in a medium bowl. Let stand for 10 minutes, until the cabbage is very wilted. Rinse and drain in a colander. A handful at a time, squeeze the cabbage and chives in your hands to extract as much liquid as possible.

2. Put the cabbage and chives in a mixing bowl. Add the ground pork and black pepper. Mix gently but thoroughly. Since the cabbage has been salted, you have to be careful with the seasoning, even though it was rinsed. To test, cook a bite of the pork mixture in a small nonstick skillet over medium heat until it is cooked through with no trace of pink, about 3 minutes. Taste and season with additional pepper to taste and salt if it's needed.

3. Have a small bowl of water at hand. Line a baking sheet with waxed paper and dust it with cornstarch. Place 1 teaspoon of the pork and cabbage filling into the center of a gyoza wrapper. Dip your finger in the water and moisten the edge of the wrapper. Bring an edge of the wrapper up over the filling to meet the other edge and form a half-moon. Press the edge of the dough firmly and fold in 6 or 7 small pleats to seal. Place on the waxed paper, plumping the bottom of the gyoza so it stands with the pleats facing up. Repeat with the remaining filling and wrappers; do not let the gyoza touch each other or they will stick together. Cover and refrigerate until ready to cook. (The gyoza can be made up to 4 hours ahead.)

4. To cook the gyoza, preheat the oven to 200°F (90°C). Heat 2 tablespoons of the oil in a 12 x 14 inch (30 x 35 cm) nonstick skillet over medium-high heat until the oil is very hot but not sizzling. Working quickly, place half of the gyoza in the skillet, pleats up, letting the gyoza touch each other at this point (gyoza are traditionally served attached to each other, but if this doesn't happen, they will still be delicious). Add 1 cup of water to the skillet and cover tightly. Cook for 5 minutes, adding more water if it evaporates before the 5 minutes is up. Cook until the water is evaporated and the gyoza are browned on the bottoms, about 7 minutes total. Invert the gyoza onto a round platter and place in the oven to keep warm. Repeat with the remaining 2 tablespoons oil and gyoza.

5. To serve, spoon about 3 tablespoons of the Rustic Tomato Sauce onto each of 8 dinner plates. Whip the Bacon-Cream Reduction with an immersion blender or hand mixer until foamy and spoon the frothy sauce around the tomato sauce. Arrange 6 gyoza, browned sides up on each plate and garnish with the remaining tablespoon of chopped chives. Serve immediately.

continued . . .

Rustic Tomato Sauce

Makes about 3 cups

This is a thick, almost jamlike sauce
with an intense flavor.

1 can (28 ounces/800 g) whole plum
tomatoes in juice

1 tablespoon extra virgin olive oil

2 garlic cloves, crushed under a knife and peeled

1 whole dried hot red pepper

½ cup finely chopped onion

2 to 3 tablespoons rendered duck fat

Salt and freshly ground black pepper

1. Drain the tomatoes, reserving the juices.
Seed the tomatoes and chop them. You can do
this easily by pulsing them in a food processor.

2. In a medium saucepan heat the oil over
medium-high heat until very hot. Add the garlic
and hot pepper and cook, stirring often, until the
garlic is golden brown. Remove and discard
the garlic and pepper.

3. Add the onion to the oil and sauté, stirring
often, until softened, about 3 minutes. Add the
chopped tomatoes and their reserved juices and
bring to a boil. Reduce the heat to medium and
cook at a brisk simmer until the sauce is thick,
about 20 minutes. Stir in the duck fat and season
with salt and pepper to taste.

**Note: The tomato sauce can be made up to 2 days
ahead; leftovers can be frozen.**

Bacon-Cream Reduction

Makes about 1 cup

1 slice of thick-cut applewood
smoked bacon, diced

2 tablespoons chopped shallot

1 cup Veal Stock (page 257)

1 sprig of fresh thyme

⅓ cup heavy cream

Freshly ground black pepper

1. Cook the bacon in a small saucepan over
medium heat until it renders its fat, about 5
minutes. Add the shallot and cook until the
shallot softens, about 2 minutes.

2. Pour in the stock, bring to a boil over high
heat, and boil until the sauce is reduced to ¾ cup,
about 5 minutes.

3. Add the cream and boil until reduced slightly
to about 1 cup, 3 to 5 minutes. Strain the sauce
through a wire sieve into a clean small saucepan.
Season with pepper to taste.

**Note: The reduction can be prepared up to 2 hours
ahead and set aside at room temperature. Reheat
before serving.**

Squid Ink-Salmon Gnocchi

and Smoked Salmon Salad with Yuzu Vinaigrette

Makes 4 servings

This dramatically colored but subtly flavored dish showcases one difficult recipe complemented by two simple ones. Each recipe can be made ahead so that final assembly is quick, easy, and drop-dead gorgeous. You will need a bamboo sushi mat to assemble the gnocchi.

12 Squid Ink-Salmon Gnocchi (recipe follows)

¼ pound (100 g) thinly smoked salmon, cut in half, if necessary to yield 12 strips

2 tablespoons sour plum powder *(yukari)*

6 cherry tomatoes, quartered

2 tablespoons chopped fresh chervil

4 tablespoons unsalted butter

1 tablespoon light-colored soy sauce

Yuzu Vinaigrette (recipe follows)

1. Prepare the Squid Ink-Salmon Gnocchi as directed on the following page. You can do this early in the day. Cook them up to 4 hours before you plan to serve.

2. Shortly before serving the gnocchi, prepare the Smoked Salmon Salad with Yuzu Vinaigrette. Roll the salmon slices into a pinwheel, then gently fold back the top edges to form a salmon rosette. Repeat until you have 12 rosettes. Dip the upper edge of each in the sour plum powder **(see photo 12 on page 71)**. Arrange 3 salmon rosettes on one side of 4 plates. Garnish with the cherry tomatoes and sprinkle with the chervil. Drizzle a small spoonful of the Yuzu Vinaigrette over the tomatoes.

3. To finish the gnocchi, heat the butter in a large sauté pan or skillet over medium-high heat, swirling the pan, just until the butter turns light brown, about 2 minutes; watch carefully so it doesn't burn. Reduce the heat to medium-low and add the gnocchi. Cook, stirring them very gently, until heated through, 2 to 3 minutes. Pour in the soy and swirl to coat. Divide gnocchi among the plates and serve immediately.

continued . . .

Squid Ink-Salmon Gnocchi

Makes 5 to 6 Servings, 35 gnocchi

8 ounces (225 g) fresh salmon fillet, skinned and cut into 1-inch (2½ cm) cubes

1 egg white

¼ cup heavy cream

1 teaspoon salt

¼ teaspoon fresh ground white pepper

2 medium Idaho potatoes
(about 1 pound/450 g total), scrubbed

1 egg yolk

1 teaspoon squid ink

½ cup all-purpose flour

Salt and freshly ground pepper

1. Purée the cubed fresh salmon and the egg white in a food processor. When the salmon is smooth, add the cream in a steady stream, then season with the salt and white pepper. Transfer the salmon mousse to a bowl, cover, and refrigerate until chilled.

2. Meanwhile, in a large saucepan of boiling salted water, cook the whole potatoes until they are tender throughout, about 30 minutes; drain and rinse under cold running water. As soon as the potatoes are cool enough to handle, peel off the skins and press the potatoes through a ricer or the medium disk of a food mill into a bowl.

3. In a small bowl, combine the egg yolk and squid ink **(photo 01)**. Beat until well blended **(photo 02)**. Add to the potato purée and mix evenly **(photo 03)**. With your hands or a wooden spoon, gradually work the flour into the potato mixture a few tablespoons at a time **(photo 04)**. Season the dough with salt and pepper to taste and divide into 5 equal portions. Gently roll each into a ball.

4. Wrap a bamboo sushi mat with plastic wrap, then poke several holes into the plastic wrap to allow air to pass through. Set the mat lengthwise in front of you and flour the mat. Place a ball of gnocchi dough on the lower third of the mat and use your fingertips to spread it out into a rectangle about ⅛-inch (3 mm) thick and about 2½-inches (6 cm) high **(photo 05)**. Leave about a 1-inch (2½ cm) margin on both sides of the mat.

5. With a ¼-inch (6 mm) plain pastry tip, pipe the salmon chilled purée horizontally across the center of the dough in a stripe about the thickness of a pencil **(photo 06)**. As if you were making sushi, roll the bottom of the mat up and over to enclose the salmon purée in the dough completely **(photo 07)**. Roll, tuck securely **(photo 08)**, and trim off any excess dough to make neat ends.

6. Unroll the mat, remove the salmon gnocchi roll, and place it in the freezer. Repeat this process with the remaining dough and salmon purée. Freeze the gnocchi for about 20 minutes, long enough so the dough is firm but not frozen.

7. Bring a large pot of salted water to a boil over high heat. Just before cooking, use a sharp knife to cut each roll into 7 pieces, each about ¾-inch (18 mm) long **(photo 09)**. Keep the knife clean by running it under cold water and wiping it dry, so the slices are neat. Add the gnocchi to the pot **(photo 10)**, reduce the heat slightly, and cook until it floats to the top, 1 to 2 minutes. As they are done, remove the gnocchi with a slotted spoon **(photo 11)**, blot briefly on paper towels, and arrange on a lightly oiled platter. The cooked gnocchi can be refrigerated, covered, for up to 4 hours.

Yuzu Vinaigrette

Makes about ½ cup

2 tablespoons *yuzu* juice (available in Asian specialty stores)

1 tablespoons rice vinegar

½ teaspoon light-colored soy sauce

1 garlic clove, minced

½ teaspoon coarse salt

¼ teaspoon coarsely ground black pepper

¼ cup grapeseed oil

Put the *yuzu* juice, vinegar, soy sauce, garlic, salt, and pepper in a mini food processor. Blend well for 20 to 30 seconds to purée the garlic. With the machine on, gradually add the oil and process until the dressing is emulsified.

Crab Naan and Bagna Cauda Morimoto-Style

Makes 4 to 6 servings

3 large heads of garlic,
cloves crushed and peeled

1 cup whole milk

⅓ cup extra virgin olive oil

2 teaspoons anchovy paste

Salt and freshly ground black
pepper

2 Japanese or ½ seedless
cucumber, cut into sticks

2 large celery sticks,
cut into sticks

8 baby carrots, peeled

8 baby *daikon*, peeled

Crab Naan

··

CRAB NAAN

Makes 4 flatbreads

2 cups all-purpose flour

½ teaspoon baking powder

½ teaspoon salt

½ cup whole milk

1 large egg

2 tablespoons plain yogurt

Olive oil

4 ounces (100 g) crab meat,
picked through for cartilage
and shells, flaked

Bagna Cauda, a hot Italian dip for vegetables, can take many forms. Some have olive oil bases; others are creamy. Two things all versions have in common are plenty of garlic and anchovies. This one is creamy and mild. I blanch the garlic several times to tame its pungency. Bagna Cauda is usually served with raw vegetables and sometimes breadsticks for dipping. I take it a step further, and accompany the dip with not just vegetables, but crab-stuffed naan, a soft Indian flatbread.

1.   To make the Bagna Cauda, bring the garlic and enough cold water to cover to boil in a medium saucepan over high heat. Drain and repeat the boiling process 2 more times.

2.   Return the boiled garlic to the saucepan and add the milk. Bring to a boil over medium heat, being sure that the milk doesn't boil over. Reduce the heat to low and simmer until the garlic is very tender, about 5 to 10 minutes. Drain the garlic through a sieve set over a bowl; reserve 1 tablespoon of the milk.

3.   In a blender or food processor, puree the garlic with the olive oil and anchovy paste, adding the 1 tablespoon of milk to make a creamy dip. Season with salt and pepper to taste. Store in a covered container in the refrigerator for up to 3 days. (Reheat before serving.)

4.   To serve, arrange the vegetables with the crab naan. Pour the warm Bagna Cauda into individual ramekins or small bowls for dipping. Serve immediately.

Crab Naan

1.   To make the naan, combine the flour, baking powder, and salt in a medium bowl. Make a well in the center and add the milk, egg, and yogurt. Mix well first to blend the wet ingredients and then to blend them with the flour to form a soft dough.

2.   Turn out onto a floured surface and knead by hand until the dough is smooth and supple, about 3 minutes. Cut the dough into 4 equal pieces. Coat your hands with oil and shape each piece into a ball. Place on the work surface, cover loosely with plastic wrap, and let stand for 30 minutes.

3.   Position racks in the top third and center of the oven and preheat the oven to 450°F (230°C). Line 2 large baking sheets with parchment.

4.   Working with 1 piece of dough at a time, on a lightly floured surface, roll out the dough into a thin, 10-inch (25 cm) long oval. Sprinkle ¼ of the crab down the center of the oval. Fold the oval in half lengthwise. Roll out the dough again to form a 10-inch (25 cm) oval. Transfer to the baking sheet. Repeat with the remaining dough and crab.

5.   Bake the crab-stuffed naan, switching the baking sheets from top to bottom halfway through baking, until the breads are spotted light brown, about 7 to 8 minutes. Serve hot or at room temperature.

71

Curry Pan

Makes 8 individual stuffed breads

Fried bread stuffed with a savory curried filling is a favorite snack or pick-up lunch in Japan. You'll find racks of these buns at Japanese bakeries and convenience stores, but this version is especially delicious. Note: The word *pan* is derived from Portuguese and they introduced yeast breads to Japan in the 1500s.

Curried Beef Filling
(recipe follows)

1 package (¼ ounce/6 g)
active dry yeast

¼ cup lukewarm water

3 cups bread flour

2 tablespoons sugar

1 teaspoon salt

2 tablespoons unsalted butter,
melted and cooled slightly

Vegetable oil, for deep-frying

1 cup all-purpose flour

4 large eggs, beaten

2 cups Japanese bread crumbs
(panko)

1. Prepare the Curried Beef Filling and chill, as directed on page 74.

2. To make the dough, sprinkle the yeast over the lukewarm water in a small bowl. Let stand for 5 minutes; then stir to dissolve the yeast.

3. In the bowl of a heavy-duty mixer, mix the flour, sugar, and salt. Add the butter and mix with the paddle attachment on low speed. Add the dissolved yeast and mix in enough cold water (about 1 cup) to make a soft dough that forms a ball on the paddle. Switch to the dough hook and knead on medium-low speed for 5 minutes. Transfer the dough to a lightly floured work surface and knead by hand until smooth and supple, about 2 minutes. (Alternately, beat the dough with a wooden spoon to mix as best you can, then turn out and knead by hand for 10 to 15 minutes.)

4. Place the ball of dough in a lightly oiled bowl and turn to coat the bowl with the oil. Cover tightly with plastic wrap and let stand in a warm place until doubled in volume, about 1 hour.

5. Punch down the dough and divide into 8 equal balls. Place the balls on a lightly oiled plate. Dust with flour, cover with plastic wrap, and refrigerate for another hour before rolling out.

6. Dust a baking sheet with flour. Working with 1 ball at a time, roll out the dough on a lightly floured work surface into a 6-inch (15 cm) round. Place 2 tablespoons of the cooled filling in the center of the round. Bring up two opposite sides of the dough to meet over the filling and pinch the seam closed to form an oval-shaped bun about 4 inches (10 cm) long. Be sure that the seam is well sealed. Place the bun seam side down on a floured baking sheet. Cover with plastic wrap while forming the remaining buns.

7. Heat the vegetable oil in a deep fryer, or at least 2 inches of oil in a large deep saucepan, to 365°F (185°C). Place the flour, beaten eggs, and *panko* in separate shallow dishes. Roll the buns in the flour, then dip in the egg, and finally in the *panko* to coat.

8. Add half the buns to the hot oil and fry, turning occasionally, until they are a deep golden brown, about 4 minutes. (After about 1 minute, spike 5 or 6 holes in each bun with a skewer to prevent them from exploding.) Do not undercook, or the dough will be soggy. Using a slotted spoon, remove the buns to a wire rack set over a baking sheet to drain. Fry the remaining buns in the same fashion. Serve the Curry Pan warm or at room temperature.

continued . . .

Curried Beef Filling

Makes about 2½ cups

1 to 2 tablespoons olive oil

8 ounces (225 g) short rib meat (cut from 1 pound/450 g short ribs) or boneless chuck, very finely chopped

1 medium onion, half thinly sliced and half grated

1 small carrot, grated

1 cup dry white wine

1 medium Idaho potato, peeled and finely diced

1½ ounces Japanese curry paste (about 1 tablespoon), available in Asian specialty stores

1 tablespoon cornstarch, dissolved in 2 tablespoons cold water, optional

Salt

1. To make the filling, heat 1 tablespoon of the olive oil in a medium skillet over medium heat. Add the beef and cook, stirring often, until browned, about 5 minutes. Using a slotted spoon, remove the beef to a plate.

2. If there is less than a tablespoon of fat left in the pan, add the remaining olive oil. Add the sliced onions and sauté over medium-high heat, stirring often, until lightly browned, about 5 minutes. Stir in the grated onion, carrot, and potato; sauté for 1 minute. Return the meat to the pan. Add the wine and bring to a boil over high heat, scraping up the browned bits from the bottom of the pan with a wooden spatula. Boil until the liquid is reduced to ½ cup, about 5 minutes.

3. Add enough water to cover the potato, about 1½ cups, and the curry paste. Bring to a boil and reduce the heat to low. Cover and simmer until the meat and potatoes are just tender, 10 to 15 minutes. Uncover, increase the heat to high, and boil, stirring occasionally, until the liquid is reduced to 1 cup, about 5 minutes.

4. If the sauce is not thick enough, stir in the dissolved cornstarch and cook until the filling is very thick, about 1 minute. Season with salt to taste. Transfer the filling to a large bowl and spread out so it can cool quickly. Then cover and refrigerate until ready to use.

Note: The filling must be cold before you fill the dough. To speed up the process, you can set the beef over a bowl of ice and water and stir occasionally until it is cool.

Dashi

Have you ever made French stock? In the sauce chapter of this book, you'll see elaborate recipes for Veal Stock and sauce Perigeux. I've browned meat and sautéed carrots, onions, and celery. I've simmered for hours, and skimmed off the flotillas of fat as they rose to the surface. Fortunately for me, *dashi*, the indispensable Japanese stock, used for everything from soups to risotto, takes about 10 minutes of active time to make and, most often, requires just two ingredients: *katsuobushi* (flakes of cured bonito) and *kombu* (kelp). Depending upon the dish they are making, cooks occasionally add dried shiitake mushrooms, *niboshi* (tiny dried anchovies), and dried mackerel. Of course, like many Japanese foods, what seems simple is, in fact, subtle and complex.

In early summer, fisherman set out in *kombu* boats to harvest the leaves from the cold, shallow waters off the coast of northern Japan, particularly near Hokkaido. They use long poles outfitted with hooks to remove the large leaves—often nearly three feet long and several inches wide—before heading back to the shore to dry the *kombu* in the sun. It comes in many different grades according to where it's harvested and how it's treated. The *kombu* you buy may be scattered with white blotches or flecks. Don't wash this off or you'll reduce *kombu's* amazing flavor-giving potential, but clean off any sand or grit with a wet towel.

Let me explain: *Kombu* does not bring a strong flavor to *dashi*, but it contributes something essential, what the Japanese call *umami*. One of the basic tastes in Japan—along with sweet, sour, salty, and bitter, *umami* refers to a less tangible quality that enhances other flavors. Its presence is felt in foods like mushrooms and meat, for example.

Why does it do this? Some of you, I'm afraid, won't like the answer, but please, bear with me. I will explain why there's nothing to worry about. *Kombu* contains a large amount of naturally occurring free glutamates—that's right, similar to MSG. In fact, *kombu*, one of the main ingredients in *dashi*,

ABOVE: **Dried whole bonito (at right) and shaved (left) in a traditional *katsuobushi* grater.**

ABOVE: **Dried shiitake mushrooms (top) and dried scallops (bottom).**

OPPOSITE: ***Kombu*, a special kelp.**

has more of this than most other foods. In it's natural form, it's not harmful in the least. Just consider a more common food that is remarkably high in this natural form of MSG: Parmesan cheese. Tomatoes are also high in free glutamate, so it's no wonder the two ingredients became such a popular tandem in Italy, each one enhancing the flavor of the other.

Another naturally occurring substance associated with *umami* is sodium inosinate. And guess what's chocked full of it? That's right, *katsuobushi*. To make it, bonito (*katsuo*), a fish with deep red meat and a flavor similar to tuna, are halved, boiled, then boned. Next it's smoked, set out in the sun to dry, and finally cured. At the end of this long process, which can take over a year, the *katsuobushi* resemble nothing so much as blocks of wood. Some vendors still sell these blocks in specialty shops in Japan, but nowadays it's much more common to find bags of wispy shaved *katsuobushi*. Machines do this job now. Cooks used to use special apparati called *katsuobushi kezuri* to shave the blocks themselves. I'm sure some still do. At my restaurants, we often shave the best quality bonito freshly over special dishes. For basic *dashi*, buy packaged bonito flakes of the best quality you can find.

Many restaurants and even many home cooks make stock using powdered *dashi*, a product similar to bouillon cubes. I make my *dashi* from scratch. When I'm in the kitchen making *dashi*, I feel exhilarated. First I wipe the *kombu* clean, without losing all the white powder as much of its flavor lies there. Then I soak the *kombu* overnight in a saucepan filled with spring water. The next day, I bring the water to the barest simmer and scatter the *katsuobushi* over the surface of the water, which produces a whiff of smokiness. I remove the pan from the heat and let it stand until the *katsuobushi* sinks to the bottom of the pan. (See page 256 for a full recipe.)

Strained, the resulting liquid is a clear stock called *ichiban dashi*, or "first dashi." I don't discard the *katsuobushi* and *kombu*—too much time and care has gone into their production; plus I've paid good money for them. Instead I use them to make a second, slightly murkier stock, called *niban dashi*, this time simmering them for a while to fully extract their flavor.

Because *ichiban dashi* offers the purest expression of ingredients, it functions as a testament to a chef's skill and is often served, more or less unadorned, as *suimono*, or clear soup. Brought to the table in a covered bowl, you remove the lid just before you eat it, sending its aroma billowing toward your nose. *Niban dashi*, whose flavor is less refined though still quite tasty, is used for miso soup, stews, and other dishes in which it plays a supporting, rather than leading, role.

Morimoto Chicken Noodle Soup

Makes 6 to 8 servings

1 frying chicken, 2½ to
3 pounds (675 g), split in half

2 teaspoons salt

1 tablespoon Sichuan
peppercorns

3 tablespoons sake

8 ounces (225 g) dried *inaniwa*
or *udon* noodles

2 quarts Shanton Broth
(page 256)

¾ cup Ramen Base

1 bunch of scallions,
green parts only, julienned

¼ cup peanut oil

....

RAMEN BASE

Makes about 1 cup

1 cup white soy sauce,
available in Asian specialty
stores

¼ cup sake

2 tablespoons salt

1 teaspoon sugar

½ cup water

1½ tablespoons vegetable oil

1 garlic clove, crushed

1 inch (2½ cm) of fresh ginger,
peeled and smashed

2 scallions, cut into 1½-inch
(4 cm) lengths

1½ teaspoons white
peppercorns

Your grandmother may make a great chicken soup, but mine is a bit more contemporary and, I'm willing to guess, a lot more interesting. Aromatic Sichuan peppercorns and a salty aromatic Ramen Base make this soup one that will surprise and delight you.

1. Place the chicken in a deep pot and pour in enough cold water to cover. Add the salt, Sichuan peppercorns, and sake. Bring to a boil, skimming off the foam as it rises to the top. Reduce the heat to a simmer and cook, uncovered, for 25 to 35 minutes, or until the chicken is completely cooked.

2. While the chicken is simmering, cook the noodles in a large saucepan of boiling water until just tender, about 1 minute, or as directed on the package. Drain and set aside.

3. As soon as the chicken is done, remove it to a colander and let stand until cool enough to handle. (The water the chicken was cooked in can be reserved for stock or discarded.) Pull the meat off the bones, removing the skin as you do so. Shred half the the chicken into bite-size pieces. Reserve the remainder for another purpose.

4. In a large saucepan, bring the Shanton Broth to a boil. Put about 1½ tablespoons of the Ramen Base into each of 6 to 8 soup bowls. Divide the cooked noodles among the bowls and pour the hot broth over the noodles. Top each bowl with a mound of shredded chicken and the julienned scallions on top of that. (The scallions should reach above the level of the broth.)

5. Quickly heat the peanut oil in a small heavy skillet until it just begins to smoke. Immediately pour 2 teaspoons of peanut oil over the scallion in each bowl and serve.

Ramen Base

Known as *men cha* in Japanese, this seasoning mixture provides instant flavor to any broth. You can make it in advance and keep it in the refrigerator for weeks.

1. Mix together the white soy sauce, sake, salt, sugar, and water.

2. In a small saucepan, combine the oil, garlic, ginger, scallions, and white peppercorns. Cook over low heat until fragrant, 2 to 3 minutes.

3. Pour the white soy mixture into the pan. Bring to a simmer and cook for 8 to 10 minutes, or until the liquid is reduced to about 1 cup. Strain before using.

Morimoto Clam Chowder

Makes 4 servings

My take on New England clam chowder uses all the classic ingredients—bacon, onion, clams, and milk—but substitutes rice for the traditional potatoes. I also puree the soup before returning the cooked clams to the base, essentially transforming the "chowder" into a rich, thick, creamy bisque.

60 Manila clams

8 slices of bacon, preferably applewood-smoked, finely chopped

½ cup finely chopped shallot

4 cups dry white wine

2 cups Scallop Congee
(page 148)

½ cup heavy cream, whipped

Salt and freshly ground white pepper

Chopped baby chives *(menegi)*, **for garnish**

1. Soak the clams in a bowl of cold salted water for 1 hour. Drain and scrub the shells to remove any loose grit.

2. Cook the bacon in a large saucepan over medium heat, stirring occasionally, until it has rendered most of its fat and is almost crisp, about 4 minutes. Add the shallot and cook until softened and translucent, about 3 minutes longer.

3. Add the clams and stir. Pour in the wine, increase the heat to high, and bring to a boil. When clams open (about 4 minutes), take 8 and set them aside, covered. Continue to cook the chowder over medium heat until reduced to ½ cup, about 45 to 60 minutes. Then discard the clams with a slotted spoon.

4. Meanwhile, purée the Scallop Congee in a food processor. Transfer to a medium saucepan and cook over medium heat until warm.

5. Add the the soup base to the Scallop Congee and stir well. Fold in the whipped heavy cream and season with salt and white pepper to taste. Divide the soup into 4 bowls and add 2 of the set-aside clams per bowl. Serve the soup hot, garnished with the chives.

Lobster Soup

Makes 4 servings

1 lobster, about 1½ pounds (625 g)

4 cups Shanton Broth
(page 256)

2 tablespoons sliced fresh ginger

Vegetable oil, for deep frying

1½ ounces (35 g) dry rice noodles

1 tablespoon Scallion Oil
(page 258)

Salt and freshly ground white pepper

2 tablespoons chopped scallions, preferably Tokyo, white parts only

***Yuzu* or lemon zest, for garnish**

Big chunks of lobster meat and one or two vegetables, which can vary depending upon the season, are presented in an elegant clear broth. This amazing liquor is the result of lobster head and shells simmered with a generous amount of fresh ginger in my meat-based Shanton Broth. What results is an intense stock, heady with lobster flavor but intriguing because of the complex base. At my restaurant, the whole soup is cooked in rice paper, a unique culinary method that prevents the soup from leaking into the small coal stove over which it's presented and cooked.

1. Split the lobster in half; remove and discard the dark "sand sack" from the head. Remove the meat from the tail and cut into bite-size pieces; reserve the shells. Break off the knuckles and claws. Poach them in a saucepan of boiling water for 3 minutes; drain. As soon as they are cool enough to handle, remove their meat and cut into bite-size pieces; add to the rest of the lobster meat. Cover and refrigerate. Split the head and coarsely chop the reserved lobster shells.

2. In a flameproof earthenware pot or enameled cast-iron casserole, bring the Shanton Broth slowly to a boil. Add the lobster head, cut-up shells, and ginger. Reduce the heat and simmer, partially covered, for 20 minutes. When the broth is nicely flavored, strain through a fine sieve and return to the saucepan.

3. In a deep fryer or large, deep saucepan, heat at last 2 inches of oil to 350°F (180°C). Add the rice noodles a handful at a time and fry until they puff, about 10 seconds. Remove with a skimmer and drain on paper towels.

4. Reheat the broth, if necessary. Add the cut lobster meat and poach over low heat for 2 to 3 minutes, or until tender and white throughout. Season with the Scallion Oil and salt and white pepper to taste.

5. With your hands, break up the fried rice noodles and divide among 4 soup bowls. Ladle the hot soup over the noodles, dividing the lobster pieces evenly. Garnish with the chopped scallions and *yuzu* zest. Serve immediately.

Silky Crab Soup

Makes 4 servings

If you have ever made consommé, you will recognize the process of clarifying broth. Unlike the "raft" of egg whites that clarifies a French consommé and is discarded, however, the seafood mousse used here both acts to clear the soup and concentrates the flavor in its silky essence, which is eaten along with the broth. In fact, the mousse becomes the centerpiece of the clear soup.

4 ounces (100 g) crab meat (jumbo lump or Dungeness), picked over to remove any bits of shell or cartilage

4 ounces (100 g) medium shrimp, peeled, deveined, and coarsely chopped

4 ounces (100 g) sea scallops, coarsely chopped

2 egg whites

¼ cup sake

1 teaspoon grated fresh peeled ginger

1 teaspoon coarse sea salt

Ground white pepper

4 cups Shanton Broth (page 256), cold

3 scallions, chopped

1. Place the crab, shrimp, and scallops in a blender or food processor and purée until smooth.

2. With the motor running, add the egg whites, sake, ginger, sea salt, and white pepper. Add the Shanton Broth to the seafood mixture in a steady stream and blend thoroughly.

3. Transfer the purée to a medium nonreactive saucepan. Cook over medium heat, stirring slowly, constantly, with a large spoon or spatula, until the liquid comes to a boil. This will take 8 to 10 minutes. Do not rush by raising the heat, or the mousse will break.

4. As soon as the broth begins to boil, stop stirring. A silky "raft" of seafood mousse will rise to the surface, leaving the broth below. Reduce the heat to a simmer and cook gently for 1 to 2 minutes, until the broth is clear.

5. Divide the seafood mousse, that is floating on the surface, into 4 parts and gently lift each into an individual soup bowl. Ladle the broth into each bowl and garnish with chopped scallions.

Mashed Potato Soup

with Wasabi and Chives

Makes 4 servings

1 large baking potato, such as Idaho or russet (10 to 12 ounces/275 to 350 g)

1½ sticks (6 ounces/175 g) unsalted butter

¾ cup half-and-half

4 cups Dashi (page 256)

2 tablespoons sake

3 tablespoons light-colored soy sauce

Salt

1 ounce (25 g) caviar, optional

Freshly grated wasabi and finely sliced chives, preferably baby chives (menegi), for garnish

I must confess I have a weakness for luxurious foods like lobster, caviar, and foie gras. But I also respect the humblest of ingredients. Their plainness offers me a different kind of challenge. Here a simple potato is transformed into an elegant soup you could serve at any dinner party. A mound of buttery mashed potatoes is surrounded with a clear broth, then garnished with fresh wasabi and chives, so every spoonful offers silky texture with bold accents.

1. Prick the potato in a couple of places. Steam over boiling water until the potato is tender when pierced with the tip of a sharp knife, 30 to 35 minutes. Let cool, then peel off the skin. Press the potato through a ricer or a wire sieve set over a medium saucepan, scraping with a rubber spatula to pass it all through.

2. In a small saucepan, combine the butter and half-and-half. Warm over medium heat until the butter melts and the liquid is steaming but not simmering.

3. Place the saucepan of mashed potatoes over low heat. Slowly whisk in the hot butter and half-and-half until the potatoes are thick and smooth. Remove from the heat and cover to keep warm.

4. Quickly bring the Dashi, sake, and soy sauce to a boil over high heat. Spoon equal amounts of the mashed potatoes into 4 soup bowls. Gently ladle the hot Dashi over and around the potatoes. Top with a spoonful of caviar if you have it. Garnish with the grated wasabi and chives. Serve immediately.

Teapot Soup with Matsutake Mushrooms

Makes 4 servings

Matsutake mushrooms are a harbinger of autumn in Japan, and during their short season, it is essential to enjoy them at least once. They are always served with reverence and in a manner that allows their unique, smoky flavor to shine, as in this very simple soup. In Japan, this is served in a special dish called a *dobin*, which is replaced with a teapot here. At the restaurant, the shrimp, mushrooms, and chicken are eaten out of the teapot and the soup is drunken out of the cup, unlike the photograph, where we've reversed it to show the ingredients.

Dobin Broth

4 large shrimp, peeled and deveined, with tail segments attached

4 *matsutake* mushrooms, wiped clean with a cloth, sliced

1 skinless, boneless chicken breast half (about 6 ounces/ 175 g), poached and diced

8 gingko nuts, preferably fresh, but canned will do

1 tablespoon *mitsuba* leaves, for garnish

2 *sudachi*, halved, or 1 lime, quartered

DOBIN BROTH

Makes 4½ cups

4 cups Dashi (page 256)

2 tablespoons sake

3 tablespoons light-colored soy sauce

Sea salt

1. Fill 4 individual teapots or 1 large teapot with boiling water and let stand to heat through. Empty the teapots and shake out excess water.

2. If it is not hot, bring the Dobin Broth to a simmer. Add the shrimp to the simmering broth and cook just until they turn pink, about 20 seconds. Using a slotted spoon, place a shrimp in each of the teapots or soup bowls. Add equal amounts of the mushrooms, chicken, and ginko nuts to each container. Pour the hot broth into the tea pots.

3. Serve the cups and pots immediately, allowing each guest to pour the hot soup into their cups. Pass the *sudachi* and *mitsuba* alongside, to season the soup with a squeeze of juice and a sprinkle of the leaves, as desired.

Dobin Broth

Bring the Dashi to a simmer in a medium saucepan over moderate heat. Add the sake and simmer for 3 minutes. Add the soy and season with sea salt to taste.

Tai Chazuke

Makes 4 servings

10 ounces (275 g) sashimi-quality red snapper, skinned and cut neatly into 16 slices

5 tablespoons sake

1 tablespoon regular soy sauce

1 tablespoon light-colored soy sauce, plus 2 teaspoons

Sesame Sauce (page 259)

1¼ cups short-grained rice

3 cups Dashi (page 256)

1 cup shredded *yaki nori* and sprigs of *mitsuba*, for garnish

Freshly grated wasabi or a dab of prepared wasabi, for garnish

Ocha means "tea" in Japanese and *zuke* means "marinated"—traditionally, this dish was made with tea, today, however, most restaurants use their own broth, as we do here. The rice is crowned with slices of red snapper *(tai)* sashimi that have been coated with a toasted sesame sauce, so the dish is called *tai chazuke.*

Note: If you have Asian sesame paste, you can mix it with a little sake to use in place of my more complex sesame sauce. Of course, the flavor will not be quite the same.

1. Combine the snapper with 2 tablespoons of the sake and the regular and light-colored soy sauces in a bowl. Cover and marinate in the refrigerator for 1 hour.

2. Meanwhile, make the Sesame Sauce and cook the rice. Rinse the rice well in a bowl of cold water, draining in a wire sieve and changing the water until it is clear. Put the rice in a small saucepan. Add 1¼ cups water and the remaining 3 tablespoons sake. Bring to a boil over high heat. Reduce the heat to low, cover, and cook until the rice is tender, about 8 minutes. Remove from the heat and let stand for 10 minutes.

3. To assemble the *tai chazuke*, bring the Dashi to a bare simmer. Remove from the heat and stir in 2 teaspoons light-colored soy sauce.

4. Divide the rice among 4 soup bowls. Drain the snapper and toss it with the Sesame Sauce. Ladle the hot Dashi over the rice. Top with the sesame-sauced snapper and garnish with the nori, *mitsuba*, and wasabi. Serve immediately.

Fish and Shellfish

Lobster Masala

Makes 4 servings

8 baby beets, preferably golden

12 baby carrots

12 asparagus stalks

½ cup broccoflower or
broccoli florets

4 live Maine lobsters,
1½ pounds (625 ounces) each

6 tablespoons olive oil,
as needed

Salt and freshly ground
white pepper

4 tablespoons Morimoto
Special Spice (page 259)

Lemon Cream

....

LEMON CREAM
Makes about 1¾ cups

1 cup heavy cream

2 teaspoons sugar

Juice of 1 lemon

Pinch of salt

Lobster Masala has become one of my signature dishes. It is seasoned with a generous coating of my Morimoto Special Spice, which provides the perfect foil for sweet, succulent lobsters. Sautéeing the lobster gives you a lot of control and intensifies the flavor. It is also quick and obviates the need for a huge pot of boiling water. You can vary the vegetable accompaniment depending upon the season.

1.   It is best to cut up the lobsters after you have prepared all the vegetables. Preheat the oven to 400°F (200°C). Wrap the beets in foil and roast for 45 minutes, or until tender. When they are cool enough to handle, rub off the skins and halve or quarter the beets.

2.   Peel the carrots and trim to leave about ½ inch (1 cm) of the green stems. Bring a large saucepan of lightly salted water to a boil. Add the carrots and cook for about 4 minutes, until just tender. Drain and rinse under cold running water.

3.   Trim the asparagus to include the tips and about 4 inches (10 cm) of the stalks. Use a swivel-blade vegetable peeler to trim off the tough skin from the thicker part of the stems. In another saucepan of boiling salted water, cook the asparagus and broccoflower until just tender, about 3 minutes.

4.   Split the lobsters lengthwise in half down the belly. Using a teaspoon, remove the dark "sand sack" from inside the head; this is the only part of the lobster that is not edible. Separate the claws with knuckles attached and crack the claws with a heavy knife. If not cooking immediately, wrap and refrigerate for no more than 2 hours. The sooner you cook the lobsters, the better.

5.   Heat 2 tablespoons of the olive oil in a very large skillet over moderately high heat. Add 2 lobsters to the skillet, meat side down, arranging the claws flat against the surface of the skillet. (If the lobsters don't fit, use 2 skillets or cook them one at a time.) Sauté until the tail meat is golden in color, 2 to 3 minutes. Turn the lobsters over and season the exposed meat of the lobster generously with 2 tablespoons of Morimoto Special Spice. Add additional oil and cover the skillet. Cook until the lobster tail meat is opaque when pierced and the shells are bright red, about 3 minutes. Remove to a platter or large plate. The claws will take 2 to 3 minutes longer. Tent the lobsters with foil to keep warm. Repeat with 2 more tablespoons of oil, the remaining 2 lobsters, and 2 more tablespoons of Morimoto Special Spice.

6.   Heat the remaining 2 tablespoons of olive oil in the same skillet. Add the cooked beets, carrots, asparagus, and broccoflowers. Toss over medium-high heat for a couple of minutes to warm through. Arrange the vegetables around the lobsters and serve with the Lemon Cream on the side.

Lemon Cream

This refreshing, simple sauce is a creamy counterpoint to the spiced lobster.

1.   In a chilled bowl, using cold beaters, whip the cream with the sugar until soft peaks form. Add the lemon juice and salt and whip until stiff.

2.   Cover and refrigerate until serving.

Lobster Chile Sauce

Makes 4 servings

At the restaurant, we use the entire lobster for this dish. For me, all those delicious juices in the legs and the green tomalley and orange roe (if you're lucky) in the body are the best part. At home, it may be easier to simply serve the big pieces of meat in the tail and save the heads and bodies for lobster stock.

2 spiny lobsters, 1 pound (450 g) each, split down the belly

½ cup vegetable oil

⅓ cup potato starch

1 ounce (25 g) Chinese vermicelli

2 tablespoons chopped fresh ginger

2 tablespoons chopped garlic

¼ cup chopped scallion

2 tablespoons Chinese chile bean paste (tobanjan)

¼ cup Chinese fermented rice pudding (chunyan)

6 tablespoons ketchup

2 tablespoons sake

1 teaspoon rice vinegar

1 tablespoon sugar

1 teaspoon coarse salt

1 teaspoon Tabasco

⅔ cup Shanton Broth or Chicken Stock (page 256)

1 tablespoon cornstarch, dissolved in 3 tablespoons water

1 tablespoon Asian sesame oil

2 tablespoons minced fresh chives, for garnish

1.   Cut the lobster tails in the shell into 1½-inch (4 cm) pieces. Reserve the heads and bodies for stock.

2.   In a large pot of boiling water, cook the tails for 2 to 3 minutes, until the shells turn red; drain. As soon as the lobster is cool enough to handle, remove the meat from the shells.

3.   In a wok or large skillet, heat ¼ cup of the oil over medium-high heat. Dust all the lobster pieces with potato starch to coat lightly. Add to the hot oil and sauté, tossing, until cooked through and golden brown, 2 to 3 minutes. With a skimmer or slotted spoon, transfer the lobster to a plate.

4.   Add the remaining ¼ cup of oil to the wok and heat to 350°F (180°C). Add the vermicelli by handfuls and fry until it puffs, about 30 seconds. Transfer to paper towels to drain.

5.   Pour out all but 2 tablespoons of oil from the wok. Add the ginger, garlic, scallion, *tobanjan*, and *chunyan*. Cook over medium-low heat, stirring, for 1 minute, or until fragrant. Add the ketchup, sake, vinegar, sugar, salt, and Tabasco. Cook, stirring, for 1 minute. Add the Shanton Broth and stir well. Thicken with the dissolved cornstarch. Return the lobster to the wok along with any juices that have collected on the plate. Cook, stirring, until the pieces are hot and coated with sauce, about 30 seconds. Stir in the sesame oil.

6.   Pile the crisp noodles on a large platter. Place the lobster and sauce over the noodles. Sprinkle the chives on top and serve immediately.

Spicy King Crab

Makes 4 to 6 servings

King crab is popular with chefs not only for its sweet, briny flavor, but because it is always a favorite with guests and is easy to eat. While we buy fresh crabs and cook them to order, you'll have even less work, because crabs are almost always sold parboiled to the consumer. Here, I help things along by removing some of the shell to expose the meat, topping it with a chile-seasoned mayonnaise, then giving it a quick glazing under the broiler. The crab ends up with a golden brown topping that is irresistible. Offer small servings as an appetizer, or one leg per person as a rich indulgence.

1 cup mayonnaise

2 tablespoons Chinese chile bean paste *(tobanjan)*

1 tablespoon Asian sesame oil

1 tablespoon fresh lemon juice

1 tablespoon fresh lime juice

2 tablespoons *tobiko* caviar

4 pounds (2 kg) king crab legs

3 tablespoons chopped fresh cilantro, for garnish

1. To make a spicy mayonnaise that coats the crab legs, combine the mayonnaise, *tobanjan*, sesame oil, lemon juice, and lime juice in a small bowl. Stir to blend well. Cover and refrigerate for up to 2 days, until ready to use. Stir in the *tobiko* caviar just before you cook the crab legs.

2. To prepare the crab, using a heavy knife, cut each leg into 4 portions at the joints. Cut the "shoulder" section in two. For each leg, you should have 2 "shoulder" portions, and 3 leg joints. Using kitchen scissors, cut off the top half of the shell of each section to expose the meat.

3. Position the broiler rack about 6 inches (15 cm) from the heat and preheat the broiler. Arrange the crab legs, meat side up, on a broiler rack or small baking sheet. Broil until the crab begins to color, 2 to 3 minutes.

4. Remove from the oven and quickly slather the mayonnaise over the crab meat to coat it liberally. Return to the broiler and broil until the mayonnaise is golden brown and bubbling, about 1½ minutes.

5. Either pile up the crab legs on a platter, or divide among 4 plates, allowing the equivalent of 1 leg per person. Garnish with a sprinkling of cilantro.

Morimoto King Crab with Black Pepper

Makes 3 to 4 servings

While I sometimes have access to fresh crab, most home cooks can buy only frozen or thawed legs that have already been cooked. Nonetheless, they should be refreshed by simmering as directed in the recipe. For the Sesame-Black Pepper Spice, it's worth going to the trouble to source Indonesian Lampong peppercorns. These have plenty of flavor as well as a pleasing bite. Lemon wedges would not be amiss as a garnish.

1½ pounds (675 g) king crab legs

1 stick (4 ounces/100 g) unsalted butter

Sesame-Black Pepper Spice

....

SESAME-BLACK PEPPER SPICE

Makes about ⅓ cup

¼ cup black sesame seeds

¼ cup whole Indonesian Lampong black peppercorns

1 tablespoon dried bonito flakes

2 teaspoons salt

1. Bring a large pot of water to a boil. Add the crab legs, reduce the heat to medium-low, and simmer for 5 minutes. Remove the crab. To make it easier to eat, as soon as the legs are cool enough to handle, trim the shells to partially expose the meat or cut them lengthwise in half.

2. Melt the butter in a sauté pan or large skillet over medium heat. Sprinkle in the Sesame-Black Pepper Spice and cook, stirring, until well blended. Add the crab legs and warm gently, turning them in the pan, until they are completely coated with the buttery spice and are heated through. Serve immediately.

Sesame-Black Pepper Spice

1. Using a spice mill, grind all the ingredients to a coarse powder.

2. Store in a covered jar in a cool, dark place for up to a month.

Morimoto Bouillabaisse

Makes 4 servings

We make this sumptuous seafood stew in *toban yaki* dishes, flameproof stoneware casseroles, but at home, you can use a large flameproof casserole. Serve right from the pot into soup plates, or divide the bouillabaisse into individual portions and present them in bowls.

2 live lobsters, 1 pound (450 g) each

2 king oyster mushrooms or large shiitake caps, sliced

16 manila clams, scrubbed

16 mussels, cleaned and debearded

8 extra-large shrimps, deveined

4 large dry, diver scallops

1 cup sake

2 cups Red Miso-Shellfish Broth (recipe follows)

2 baby bok choy, quartered

1 tablespoon unsalted butter

Salt and freshly ground black pepper

Zest of a fresh *yuzu* or lemon

1. In a large pot of boiling water, cook the lobsters for 3 to 5 minutes, until they are red and no longer moving. Remove the lobsters. As soon as they are cool enough to handle, split the lobsters in half. Remove the dark "sand sack" from the heads of the lobsters. Loosen the tail meat, leaving it in the shell, and crack the claws.

2. Arrange the sliced mushrooms in the bottom of a large flameproof casserole. Add a layer of clams, then mussels, shrimp, lobsters, and scallops. Pour in the sake, cover the pan, and set over high heat. Bring to a boil and cook for 2 minutes to allow the alcohol in the sake to burn off.

3. Pour in the Red Miso-Shellfish Broth, cover again, and bring to a simmer. Cook for 2 minutes.

4. Add the baby bok choy and butter. Season the sauce with salt and pepper to taste. Cover and bring just to a boil. By now, the shellfish should have opened and the lobster meat should be opaque and tender. If not, reduce the heat and simmer for 2 minutes longer. Discard any clams or mussels that do not open.

5. Sprinkle the zest over the top and serve from the pot or divide among large soup bowls or rimmed plates, making sure everyone gets an assortment of each kind of seafood and the baby bok choy. Ladle the broth over all.

continued . . .

Red Miso-Shellfish Broth

Makes about 6 cups

2 tablespoons olive oil

1 medium leek (white and pale green parts), coarsely chopped

2 medium carrots, peeled and coarsely chopped

1 small fresh fennel bulb, coarsely chopped

2 shallots, coarsely chopped

½ cup tomato paste

1½ cups dry white wine

6 cups Lobster Broth (page 258)

6 cups Fish Fumet (page 258)

½ cup red miso (available in Asian specialty stores)

½ cup Korean chile paste *(kochujan)*

1. Heat the olive oil in a large stockpot. Add the leek, carrots, fennel, and shallots. Cover and cook over low heat, stirring once or twice, until the vegetables are soft, 7 to 10 minutes.

2. Add the tomato paste, raise the heat to moderate and cook, stirring, for 2 minutes. Pour in the white wine and bring to a boil. Boil until the wine is reduced by half, about 5 minutes.

3. Add the Lobster Broth and Fish Fumet. Bring to a boil, reduce the heat to a simmer, and cook until the liquid is reduced by half, about 45 minutes.

4. In a heatproof bowl, whisk together the red miso and *kochujan*. Whisk about 1 cup of the hot broth into the mixture until well blended. Then stir the miso-*kochujan* mixture into the remaining broth in the stockpot; this process ensures all the paste gets dissolved into the broth. Simmer 5 minutes longer.

5. Strain the broth. Let cool, then cover and refrigerate for up to 3 days, or freeze for longer storage.

Plating and Presentation

In Japanese, there is a word for the way chefs arrange food on plates: *moritsuke*. The word also refers to the principles that guide the arrangement. Based on these, certain styles of presentation developed, such as *sugimori*, in which chefs mound ingredients in the shape of an upside-down cone so it resembles a cedar tree, and *tawaramori*, in which chefs stack food in a pyramid, as farmers stack rice bales.

I have my own way of dealing with these formal rules and styles: I often ignore them. Some Japanese chefs are shocked at my lack of regard for tradition, but because I serve customers of many different backgrounds, not just Japanese, I must serve food that resonates beyond just one culture.

The first experience a customer has with a plate of my food is a visual one. I must make sure each plate of food is impressive, dramatic. Though Japanese food's popularity has skyrocketed in the last decade, there are plenty of people, even in cosmopolitan cities such as New York and Los Angeles, who are not entirely comfortable with the cuisine. They're squeamish about raw fish, perhaps, or reluctant to try octopus. While it is ultimately my duty to seduce them with aroma and taste, first I must entice them with colors and visual textures, to make the food so beautiful they cannot resist trying it.

I also use presentation to distinguish my food from everyone else's. Nowadays, countless Japanese restaurants serve Toro Tartare (see page 194), a new-style dish that I have made for many years. I wanted my version to stand out, so after carefully considering the flavors, I went to work on making it exceptionally beautiful. At my restaurants, very finely minced fatty tuna (the toro tartare), is spread out in a shallow, rectangular wooden box so that its pale, almost iridescent pink color is framed by the blond wood barrier. Next to this, another small wooden container holds stripes of multi-colored condiments, among them blackish nori purée, pale green wasabi, white sour cream, and beige spheres of miniature rice crackers. Against a snowy backdrop of crushed ice, the visual is striking and exciting. Diners can't wait to dip into the fatty tuna, then swipe their spoons through the palette of condiments, adding a bit of spice, sweetness, or crunch to the rich fish, according to their whim.

I like food that encourages people to participate in what they're eating. My signature Morimoto Sashimi (see page 194), little stacks comprising five layers of different fish,

Plating and Presentation

come not just with fresh wasabi, but also with five squeezable tubes, each containing a different brightly colored sauce made from ingredients like arugula, *yuzu*, or red pepper.

Of course, you might notice that though my plating is distinctively original, it does often draw inspiration from the Japanese aesthetic. After all, I am Japanese. My notion of what is attractive has been shaped by years of seeing the principles of food arrangement in action, so I can't help but incorporate the basics, purposefully as well as subconsciously, into my design.

For instance, you may notice that on my plates there is typically a lot of empty space. In comparison to the dishes plated by many Western chefs, who tend to fill every inch with meat, sauce, vegetable, and grain, my presentations are often spare—a slice of fish, a streak of sauce, a tiny bundle of greens all clustered in the center of the plate. The negative space frames my arrangement, focusing your attention. My minimalism is visually pleasing, but it also symbolizes an important culinary principle that guides my cuisine: Everything that would detract from my food has been omitted, edited out.

In addition, like many other more traditional Japanese chefs, I value asymmetry and contrast. These are two of the characteristics that breathe life into a specific

presentation, electrifying it. Symmetry is tempting. Imagine a slice of raw fish topped with greens and encircled by sauce. It's superficially attractive, eye-catching but not engaging. Instead, I avoid the predictable, preferring the off-center and the irregular. To maximize contrast, I match black plates with stark white squid; I pair silvery shad gizzard with bright orange sea urchin.

This does not mean that the arrangements on my plates are jarring, filled with random splotches of color and arranged willy-nilly. My application of asymmetry and contrast take more subtle forms. For example, I don't place pieces of sushi so that they're parallel with the sides of a rectangular dish. This would be uninteresting to the eye; it would dull the visual experience. Instead, I place them diagonally, stimulating the mind and drawing more attention to the pale, shimmering colors of the fish.

Joining me and my talented top chefs for an *omakase*, or "chef's choice," dinner brings the best opportunity to see my style of plating in action. Your meal is entirely in our hands, which gives us the chance not only to exhibit a wide variation of presentation styles but also to compose a meaningful procession, with each course's appearance relating to the one before it.

ABOVE: **These five squeezable tubes, containing different sauces for my Morimoto Sashimi, add some fun to dipping.**

LEFT: **These three sushi pieces (*kurumba ebi*, *shikai maki*, and *uni*) show the skill involved in presenting sushi to both the novice and experienced eater.**

RIGHT: **My Appetizers with 10 Tastes (see page 224) is a rare form of presentation.**

Rock Shrimp Tempura

Makes 4 servings

Rock shrimp are especially sweet and tender. If they're not available in your market, use the freshest, cleanest smelling shrimp you can find.

Vegetable oil, for deep frying

¾ pound (350 g) rock shrimp or other small shrimp, shelled and deveined

2 tablespoons all-purpose flour

2 cups Tempura Batter (page 260)

Wasabi Aioli

Spicy Mayonnaise

¼ cup minced fresh chives

Ranch Dressing

4 celery ribs, cut into 3-inch (7 cm) sticks

2 Japanese cucumbers, or 3 Kirby cucumbers, peeled and cut into 3-inch (7 cm) sticks

1. Heat at least 2 inches of vegetable oil in a deep-fryer or large heavy saucepan to 350°F (180°C) or smoking.

2. Pat the shrimp very dry on paper towels. Divide into 2 equal portions and set aside.

3. Place one half of the shrimp in a bowl and sprinkle with 1 tablespoon of the flour. Toss the shrimp to coat lightly but thoroughly. Place the Tempura Batter in a second bowl and dip the 2nd portion of shrimp until each is well coated.

4. Using a large, long-handled spoon, carefully add the battered shrimp to the hot oil in 3 batches; avoid any splashing hot oil. With a wire mesh skimmer or chopsticks, gently stir the shrimp to separate. As they cook, continue to stir carefully, moving the shrimp around so they cook evenly. Fry for 3 to 4 minutes, until the shrimp are crisp but not browned. With a skimmer or slotted spoon, transfer to paper towels and drain well. Coat and fry the remaining shrimp in the same way.

5. In a small bowl, toss half the hot fried shrimp with the Wasabi Aioli to coat generously. Sprinkle with half the minced chives.

6. In another bowl, toss the remaining fried shrimp with the Spicy Mayonnaise and garnish with the remaining chives. Serve both batches of shrimp immediately with the celery and cucumber sticks and Ranch Dressing for dipping.

WASABI AIOLI
Makes about 1¼ cups

¼ cup sugar

1 tablespoon fresh lemon juice

1 teaspoon gin

1 cup mayonnaise

2 tablespoons wasabi paste

1 tablespoon sweetened condensed milk

In a mixing bowl, whisk together the sugar, lemon juice, and gin. Add the mayonnaise, wasabi paste, and sweetened condensed milk and whisk until well blended. Cover and refrigerate until serving time.

RANCH DRESSING
Makes about 1 cup

½ cup buttermilk

½ cup sour cream

1 tablespoon chopped fresh dill

1 tablespoon white wine vinegar

1 tablespoon fresh lemon juice

1 teaspoon garlic powder

½ teaspoon salt

Combine all the ingredients and stir to mix well. Cover and refrigerate until serving.

SPICY MAYONNAISE
Makes about 1 cup

1 cup mayonnaise

1 tablespoon Korean chile paste (kochujan)

1 tablespoon sweetened condensed milk

1 tablespoon lemon juice

1 tablespoon sugar

1 tablespoon dried crushed hot pepper flakes, preferably Korean

1 teaspoon Grand Marnier

1 teaspoon salt

Combine all the ingredients and stir to mix well. Cover and refrigerate until serving.

Fish and Shellfish

Morimoto Tempura

Makes 4 servings

2 large sea scallops, about 3½ ounces (90 g) total

1 tablespoon egg white*

2 teaspoons heavy cream

Salt

8 large fresh shiitake mushrooms, 1½ to 2 inches (5 cm) in diameter, stemmed

All-purpose flour, for dusting

8 medium-large shrimp, peeled and deveined

4 ounces (100 g) skinless red snapper fillet, cut into 4 strips about 3-inches (5 cm) long and ¾-inches (5 cm) wide

4 slices of fresh lotus root, ¼-inch (6 mm) thick

4 asparagus tips, 3-inches (5 cm) long

4 rounds of Japanese eggplant, cut about ½-inch (1 cm) thick

4 baby carrots

4 slices of Japanese yams, ¼-inch (6 mm) thick

1-inch (2½ cm) cube of mozzarella, wrapped in 1 slice of bacon

Vegetable oil, for deep-frying

4 cups Tempura Batter (page 260)

Gorgonzola Sauce

*Beat a large egg white until foamy; measure out 1 tablespoon and discard the rest.

GORGONZOLA SAUCE

Makes about 1¼ cups

1 cup heavy cream

2 ounces (50 g) Gorgonzola Dolce cheese, crumbled (about ½ cup)

2 teaspoons potato starch

1 teaspoon light-colored soy sauce

Ground white pepper

Part of the appeal of tempura is serving a variety of ingredients. In my special tempura, I include shiitake mushrooms stuffed with scallop mousse, white fish, and shrimp, along with an assortment of tempting vegetables—all served with a Gorgonzola Sauce for dipping.

One caveat: Do not drain the tempura on paper towels, because wherever the batter touches a surface, steam will collect and soften the crunchy crust. If drained on a wire rack, the air will circulate around the tempura, keeping it light and crisp.

1. To make the stuffed shiitake, pulse the scallops in a food processor until chopped. With the machine on, slowly add the egg white and heavy cream in a thin stream, and season with salt to taste. Continue to process until the mousse is smooth. Spoon the mousse into the shiitake, mounding it up and smoothing the top.

2. Pour the flour into a 9 x 13 inch (22½ x 32½ cm) baking dish. Dip the stuffed shiitake, shrimp, fish strips, lotus root, asparagus, eggplant, carrots, yams, and mozzarella in the flour to coat lightly; shake off any excess. Skewer the ingredients on to individual (10-inch/25 cm) bamboo skewers. Set the skewers aside on a baking sheet.

3. Preheat the oven to 200°F (90°C). Place a wire cake rack on a rimmed baking sheet. Pour enough vegetable oil into a 12 x 14 inch (30 x 35 cm) skillet or a large wok to reach about ¾ inch (2 cm) up the sides. Heat the oil over high heat to 375°F (190°C).

4. Meanwhile, mix the Tempura Batter as directed. One at a time, dip 2 skewers into the batter, letting the excess batter drip back into the dish. Add to the hot oil and fry, basting the top of the skewer with the hot oil and turning once, until golden on both sides, about 3 minutes. Transfer to the wire rack and keep warm in the oven while frying the remaining 2 skewers, being sure to let the oil return to 375°F (190°C) before adding them.

5. Divide the warm Gorgonzola Sauce among 4 ramekins or small bowls. Serve immediately, with the sauce for dipping

Gorgonzola Sauce

1. Bring the cream to a simmer in a small saucepan over medium heat. Add the Gorgonzola and whisk until smooth; return to a simmer.

2. Sprinkle the potato starch over 1 tablespoon cold water in a small bowl and stir to dissolve. Whisk into the hot Gorgonzola cream and simmer until the sauce thickens lightly, about 20 seconds. Add the soy sauce and season with white pepper to taste. Remove from the heat and keep warm until serving.

Striped Bass Vongole

Makes 4 servings

Here raw slices of fish, barely poached in a bath of flavorful white wine–shellfish broth, are topped with clams, mussels, octopus, and shrimp.

12 ounces (300 g) sashimi-quality striped bass, thinly sliced

1½ tablespoons olive oil

1 shallot, minced

1 garlic clove, minced

2 cups dry white wine

12 mussels

12 manila clams

8 extra-large shrimp, shelled and deveined

3 ounces (75 g) octopus, thinly sliced, optional

4 tablespoons unsalted butter

2 tablespoons light-colored soy sauce

2 tablespoons chopped parsley

Salt and freshly ground black pepper

1. Arrange the slices of striped bass in a circular pattern like flower petals in 4 large shallow bowls.

2. In a large sauté pan or skillet, heat the olive oil over medium heat. Add the shallot and garlic and cook until softened and translucent, about 3 minutes.

3. Pour in the wine and bring to a boil, then add the mussels and clams. Cover and steam until the shells just begin to open, 2 to 3 minutes. Add the shrimp, octopus, butter, and soy sauce and cook until the shrimp are pink and curled and the shells are open. Discard any clams or mussels that do not open.

4. With a slotted spoon, transfer the seafood to the center of the serving dish, leaving the fish exposed around the rim. Strain the cooking liquid through several thicknesses of cheesecloth into a medium saucepan. Bring to a boil and cook until the liquid is reduced to 1 cup. Season the sauce with salt if it needs it, and with pepper to taste.

5. Pour about ¼ cup of broth over the fish. The hot broth will cook the thinly sliced fish. Sprinkle with the parsley and serve immediately.

Braised Black Cod

Makes 6 servings

You have probably seen this popular classic or tasted it before. The biggest secret of success here is finding pristinely fresh black cod, also known as sable fish. It is a rich, oily fish that takes well to the dark sweet sauce. This fish is native to the Pacific, so it is not as common on the East Coast.

2 cups sake

6 slices of fresh ginger

6 black cod fillets with skin on, 6 to 7 ounces (175 to 200 g) each

1½ cup sugar

1 cup soy sauce

1½ teaspoons tamari

3 tablespoons mirin

....

VEGETABLE RAGOUT

Serves 6

1 carrot, peeled and diced on an angle

1 bamboo shoot (about 8 ounces/225 g), rinsed if canned, diced

8-inch (20 cm) piece of burdock root, peeled and diced on an angle

6 dried shiitake mushrooms, rehydrated, stem-cleaned, and quartered

½ yam cake, diced with a spoon

2 tablespoons Asian sesame oil

½ cup soy sauce

¼ cup sake

1½ cups Chicken Stock (page 256)

⅓ cup sugar

Julienned Tokyo scallion and ginger, for garnish

Sprigs of *kinome*, for garnish

1. Pour the sake into a large, deep skillet or flame-proof casserole. Add the ginger and fish fillets skin side up. Cover and cook over high heat for 3 minutes. Add the sugar and cook over medium-high heat for 3 more minutes.

2. Pour the soy sauce and tamari over the fish fillets. Cook over medium-high heat, covered, for 5 minutes. Add the mirin and cook for 3 minutes longer. Be careful not to burn the fish; glaze the fillets by repeatedly pouring the thickened sauce over them while cooking.

3. With a slotted spatula, carefully transfer the black cod fillets to a platter. Check the fish to make sure it has no residual bones hidden in it.

4. If the braising liquid is not thick enough, keep cooking it over high heat until it becomes caramalized.

5. Garnish the cod with the julienned scallion and ginger and sprigs of *kinome*, and drizzle with the braising liquid.

Vegetable Ragout

1. Bring a large pot of water to a boil. Set a large bowl of ice and water next to the stove. One at a time, blanch your vegetables for 2 minutes. Drain well. (The vegetables can be prepared several hours in advance.)

2. Heat the sesame oil in a large skillet. Add the vegetables and sauté over medium heat until tender and lightly browned about 3 minutes.

3. Add the soy sauce, sake, Chicken Stock, and sugar. Simmer, stirring occasionally, until the vegetables are just tender, about 30 minutes.

Snapper Chips

Makes 4 servings

10 ounces (275 g)
red snapper fillet

½ cup potato starch

Vegetable oil

Guacamole Sauce

....

GUACAMOLE SAUCE
Makes about 1 cup

1 avocado, peeled, pitted, and
quartered

1 teaspoon fresh grated wasabi

1 pinch salt

Dash of light-colored soy
sauce

1 tablespoon chopped fresh
cilantro leaves

1 jalapeño, minced

1 tablespoon *sudachi* juice

Here's my answer to potato chips and
dip: paper-thin slices of red snapper,
fried until crisp and served with a tasty
Guacamole Sauce.

1. Choose very fresh fish with tight shiny skin **(photo 01)**. Place the fish skin side down and run your fingers over the flesh to make sure there are no pin bones. Peel the skin off carefully. On an angle using a very sharp knife, cut the fish into thin slices **(photo 02)**.

2. Place a sheet of plastic wrap on your work surface. Sprinkle with a little of the potato starch. Arrange several slices of snapper, leaving room between them, and sprinkle with a little more of the starch. Place another sheet of plastic wrap over the fish and pound with a wooden mallet or the smooth side of a meat pounder **(photo 03)**. Without tearing the fish, pound until the slices are as thin as possible **(photo 04)**. The slices should be so translucent you can almost see through them **(photo 05)**.

3. In a heavy deep saucepan, heat at least 2 inches (5 cm) of vegetable oil to 340°F (170°C). In batches of two or three without crowding, dredge the fish slices in the remaining potato starch to coat both sides and add to the hot oil **(photo 06)**. Fry until light golden brown, about 2 minutes, and let cool. Then fry for another 2 minutes, to make them extra crispy. Drain briefly on paper towels. Serve immediately with a bowl of Guacamole Sauce for dipping.

Guacamole Sauce

Place all of the ingredients in a food processor and purée to desired consistency.

01

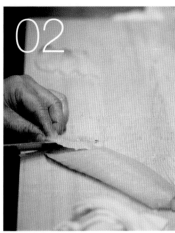

02

03

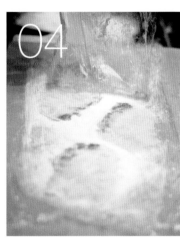

04

05

06

117

Grilled Scallop-Stuffed Sweet Onion

Makes 4 servings

Here, just a few ingredients, each perfectly prepared to bring out their natural sweetness, are combined into an extraordinary dish. Whole sweet onions are slow-roasted until meltingly tender, then stuffed with a seared proscuitto-wrapped scallop. The result is a combination of sweet and salty in a striking presentation. While the quality of your ingredients is always important, this dish really shines when made with diver, or day-boat, scallops, which, unlike average scallops, have not been treated with chemical preservatives, and fine imported prosciutto di Parma.

4 large sweet onions, such as Vidalia, Maui, or Walla Walla, (about 7 ounces/200 g) each

2 tablespoons olive oil

Salt and freshly ground black pepper

½ cup sake

4 very large diver or day-boat "dry" sea scallops, preferably U-10 size

4 thin slices of prosciutto

2 tablespoons unsalted butter

1. Preheat the oven to 325°F (160°C). Place the onions in their skins in an 11½ x 8 inch (28 x 20 cm) metal baking pan. Rub the onions with the oil, and season all over with salt and pepper. Cover the pan tightly with aluminum foil. Roast until the onions are very tender but still hold their shape, about 2½ hours. Transfer the onions to a platter and let stand until cool enough to handle.

2. Place the baking pan over high heat on the stove. Add the sake to the pan and scrape up the browned onion juices with a wooden spatula. Pour this onion jus into a bowl and set aside.

3. Cut off the top third of the onions and reserve. Remove the center of each onion to make a hole large enough to hold a scallop.

4. Season the scallops with salt and pepper and wrap each in a piece of prosciutto to enclose completely.

5. Prepare a hot fire in an outdoor grill and lightly oil the grill grate, or preheat a grill pan on top of the stove. In a small saucepan, reheat the onion jus, season with salt and pepper to taste, and keep warm.

6. Grill the scallops, turning once, just until the prosciutto is seared with brown marks, about 30 seconds on each side; do not overcook, as they will be cooked further. Stuff a scallop into each onion, top each with ½ teaspoon of butter, cover with the reserved onion top, and place on the grill or grill pan.

7. Grill the onions for 6 to 8 minutes, or until they are heated through and the skin burns black (as shown in photo). Place an onion on each of 4 plates and peel off the burnt skin. Take off the onion tops and drizzle the onion jus over the scallops. Serve immediately.

Fried Fish Cake Noodles

Makes 4 servings

10 ounces (275 g) striped bass or other white fish fillet, plus bones, head, and tail from fish

½ cup salt

1 egg white

2 tablespoons cornstarch

2 tablespoons finely grated Japanese mountain potato

¼ cup sake

Freshly ground white pepper

4 x 3-inch (7 cm) pieces of *kombu*

1 fresh jalapeño pepper, seeded and thinly sliced

3 tablespoons vegetable oil

3 tablespoons light-colored soy sauce

2 tablespoons chopped Tokyo scallion (white part only)

4 sprigs of fresh cilantro, for garnish

1 tablespoon Japanese black seven-spice *(kuro-shichimi)*, available in Asian specialty stores, or freshly ground black pepper

You may wonder why this recipe is here rather than in the Rice, Noodles, Breads, and Soups chapter. Well, my fondness for visual puns may give you a hint. These are not true noodles at all, but rather a delicate fish cake, or purée, which is poached in long narrow strands to make it resemble noodles and then fried until crispy. Served in a bowl with chile-spiked fish broth and topped with shredded scallion, the preparation looks very much like traditional Japanese noodles in Dashi.

1. Cure the fish with the salt and let sit for 30 minutes **(photo 01)**. Rinse the fish under running water to remove the salt and pat dry with paper towels. Cut the fish fillet into 1-inch (2½ cm) pieces. In a food processor, combine the fish with the egg white, cornstarch, mountain potato, 2 tablespoons of the sake, ½ teaspoon of salt, and a pinch of white pepper. Purée until smooth. Transfer the fish purée to a bowl, cover, and refrigerate while you make the broth.

2. Place the fish bones, head, and tail in a large saucepan of boiling water. After 20 seconds, drain. Add 4 cups of water and 2 pieces of *kombu* and cook over medium-low heat for 30 minutes. Strain the fish broth and set aside **(photo 02)**.

3. In a clean large saucepan, warm the oil over medium heat. Add the jalapeño and cook for 30 to 60 seconds, until just softened **(photo 03)**. Add the remaining 2 tablespoons sake (being careful that the hot oil does not splatter you), then pour the fish broth into the pot. Simmer for 5 minutes. Add the light-colored soy sauce, the remaining 1 teaspoon of salt, and white pepper to taste. Set the seasoned fish broth aside.

4. Bring a large pot of water and the remaining 2 pieces of *kombu* to a boil; reduce the heat to a simmer and discard the *kombu*. Put the chilled fish purée in a piping bag fitted with a ¼-inch (6 mm) plain tip. Holding the tip over the center of the pot, pipe ¼ of the fish purée in concentric circles to form a large coil, like a sausage **(photos 04 and 05)**. Poach gently for 20 to 30 seconds, or until the fish "noodle" is firm.

5. Using a wide slotted spatula, gently remove the "noodle" from the poaching water and drain on paper towels. Repeat 3 more times with the remaining fish purée.

6. In a large wide saucepan, heat about 1 inch (2½ cm) of vegetable oil until it registers 350°F (180°C). Add the "noodles" one coil at a time **(photo 06)**, and lightly fry the fish noodles until pale golden brown, 1 to 2 minutes. Be sure to allow the oil to return to temperature between batches.

7. As they are done, transfer the fish noodles to paper towels to drain **(photo 07)**. Divide the fish noodles among 4 soup bowls and top with the seasoned fish broth, scallions, cilantro, and *kuro-shichimi* **(photo 08)**.

Oyster Foie Gras

Makes 4 servings

At my restaurant, as you can see in the photo, we serve a slab of sautéed foie gras over a special giant oyster. At home, I recommend cubes of foie gras on top of buttery *Kunomoto* oysters, which are small.

2 tablespoons sake

2 tablespoons soy sauce

2 tablespoons mirin

2 tablespoons sugar

1½ teaspoons cornstarch

6 ounces (175 g) fresh foie gras, cut ½- to ¾-inch (20 mm) thick

Freshly ground black pepper

12 pieces of *uni* (about 4 ounces/100 g)

4 Pacific jumbo oysters, freshly shucked

4 sprigs of fresh chervil or parsley, for garnish

1. In a small bowl, make a teriyaki sauce by combining the sake, soy sauce, mirin, and sugar. In another small bowl, dissolve the cornstarch in 2 tablespoons of water.

2. Heat a small dry, heavy skillet over high heat until very hot. Cut the foie gras into 4 pieces, season with pepper, and add to the hot pan. Sear quickly on both sides until browned outside and warmed through but still rare, 60 seconds on each side. Remove to a plate.

3. Reduce the heat to medium. Pour the teriyaki sauce into the skillet and scrape up the browned bits from the bottom of the pan. Add the dissolved cornstarch and stir until thickened and smooth. Immediately remove from the heat.

4. In a steamer over boiling water, place 3 pieces of *uni* on top of each oyster and steam for 3 minutes, until just cooked.

5. Transfer the *uni*-oysters to 4 plates and top each with a slice of foie gras. Drizzle the thickened teriyaki sauce over the oysters and foie gras. Garnish each with a sprig of chervil. Serve immediately.

Orange-Roasted Seafood

and *Kunomoto* Oysters with White Miso Sauce

Makes 4 servings

4 navel oranges

1 bunch of scallions, roots and ends trimmed

8 *Kunomoto* oysters, freshly shucked

1 pound (450 g) fresh squid, bodies only, no tentacles, cut into thin strips

4 large shrimp, shelled and deveined

1 cup White Miso Sauce (page 259)

Depending upon my mood or what I'm trying to effect, sometimes I use flavors boldly and sometimes subtly. Here fresh seafood, mixed with White Miso Sauce and scallions, is baked in a shell of scooped-out orange. In my restaurant, I serve the oysters and squid in separate oranges, as shown.

1. Cut off the top ⅓ of each orange. Use a curved grapefruit knife to scoop out the insides of the oranges. Reserve the pulp for a fruit salad or other use. Reserve the orange shell to use as a cooking vessel.

2. Bring a medium skillet of salted water to a simmer. Add the scallions and cook for 30 seconds. With tongs, rinse the scallions under cold running water; pat dry on paper towels. Holding the root ends, run the back of a large knife down the length of the scallions, pressing down to squeeze out as much liquid as possible. Slice into 1-inch (2½ cm) pieces.

3. In the same skillet, slip the oysters, squid, and shrimp into the water and poach over low heat until the edges of the oysters curl, 10 to 15 seconds. Immediately transfer to a bowl; do not overcook.

4. Pour 2 tablespoons of the White Miso Sauce into each orange shell. Spoon the seafood mixture in next, mounding as needed. Finally, top with another 2 tablespoons of the White Miso Sauce.

5. Preheat the oven to 400°F (200°C). Bake the seafood-stuffed oranges for 10 minutes, or until hot throughout. Transfer to individual plates and serve immediately.

White Nuta

Makes 4 small servings

In some Japanese homes, a small bowl of White Nuta often accompanies other dishes in a main meal, as it is a light and savory dish.

WHITE NUTA

½ pound (225 g) fresh squid, bodies only, no tentacles

2 bunches of scallions, roots trimmed

½ cup White Miso Sauce (page 259)

2 teaspoons rice vinegar

2 teaspoons Japanese spicy yellow mustard

....

RED NUTA

½ pound (225 g) very fresh sashimi-quality tuna

2 bunches of scallions, roots trimmed

½ cup Red Miso Sauce (page 259)

2 teaspoons rice vinegar

1 tablespoon white sesame seeds

1. Rinse the squid well. Cut crosswise into rings about ⅜-inch (9 mm) wide. Have a bowl of water with ice near the stove.

2. Bring 3 cups of water to a boil in a small saucepan. Add the squid and cook for 15 seconds, just until the squid turns opaque. Immediately remove the squid with a slotted spoon and plunge it into the ice water. Reserve the poaching liquid. Drain the squid rings and pat dry.

3. Return the poaching liquid to a boil. Holding the whole scallions with your fingers, lower the white bulbs into the reserved boiling water and cook for 20 to 30 seconds, or until softened. Turn them upside down and dip the green part of the scallions into the pot for 5 to 10 seconds, just until wilted. Drop them into a bowl of ice water or rinse under cold running water to cool.

4. Drain the scallions and pat them dry, and press out any excess liquid. Using the back of a large chef's knife, press firmly on the green part of the scallion and run the knife down its length to squeeze out as much liquid as possible. Cut the scallions into 1-inch (2½ cm) lengths.

5. In a medium bowl, combine the White Miso Sauce, the rice vinegar, and the mustard. Add the squid rings and scallions and toss to coat. Serve in a small bowl.

Red Nuta

Makes 4 small servings

Like white nuta, red nuta is a mixture of miso sauce and scallions. In this case, I've added squid and sesame seeds.

1. In a medium saucepan, bring 3 cups of water to a boil. Have a bowl of water with ice near the stove. Add the tuna and cook only until the surface loses its raw color, about 10 seconds. With a slotted spatula or spoon, remove the fish and plunge it into the bowl of ice and water to stop the cooking immediately. Reserve the cooking liquid.

2. As soon as the fish is cool enough to handle, drain it and pat dry. Cut the fish into ¾-inch (2 cm) cubes.

3. Return the poaching liquid to a boil. Holding the whole scallions with your fingers, lower the white bulbs into the reserved boiling water and cook for 20 to 30 seconds, or until softened. Turn them upside down and dip the green part of the scallions into the pot for 5 to 10 seconds, just until wilted. Drop them into a bowl of ice water or rinse under cold running water to cool.

4. Drain the scallions and pat them dry. Using the back of a large chef's knife, press firmly on the green part of the scallion and run the knife down its length to squeeze out as much liquid as possible. Cut into 1-inch (2½ cm) lengths.

5. In a medium bowl, combine the Red Miso Sauce with the rice vinegar, stirring to mix well. Add the fish cubes and scallions and toss to coat. Transfer to a small bowl and sprinkle the sesame seeds on top.

Duck, Chicken, Pork, Beef, and Lamb

Crispy Duck with Port Wine Reduction and Red Miso Sauce

Makes 4 servings

One of my most famous dishes is called Duck, Duck, Duck. Inspired by Peking Duck, it takes the recipe to another level. The leg and thigh of the meltingly tender duck with its lacquered crisp skin is served with an intense Port Wine Reduction as well as an earthy Red Miso Sauce for dipping. Alongside it are a "sandwich," the sliced breast meat from the duck tucked with scallions inside a Foie Gras Croissant and a sunny-side-up duck egg, the third duck." Be sure to begin preparation of the duck at least two days before you plan to serve it—it is the special dipping and drying technique that gives the duck its glazed skin. Each serving could easily feed two people.

2 ducks, about 4½ pounds (2 kg) each

6 tablespoons Five-Spice Powder (page 259)

½ cup coarse salt

1 jar (8 ounces/225 g) millet jelly, or ¾ cup light corn syrup

1 cup red wine vinegar

Port Wine Reduction (recipe follows)

Red Miso Sauce (page 259)

Foie Gras Croissants (recipe follows)

4 duck eggs, fried sunny-side-up, optional

1. At least 2 days before serving, rinse the duck inside and out. Pull out all the excess fat from the area near the tail, and cut off the excess skin. (You can reserve these pieces, chop them up, and cook in a small saucepan over very low heat to render the fat for another use.) Pat the duck completely dry with paper towels.

2. Mix the Five-Spice Powder and salt, and rub all over the inside and outside of the duck. Place the duck on a wire rack set over a baking sheet. Refrigerate, uncovered, for 24 hours.

3. The next day, rinse the duck, and wash and dry the rack and baking sheet. Bring 8 quarts (8 liters) of water to a boil in a stockpot large enough to hold the duck. Add the millet jelly and vinegar. Tie a string around the duck's legs and dip the duck 10 times into the boiling solution. Return the duck to the rack on the baking sheet, let cool, then refrigerate uncovered for at least 24 hours and up to 48 hours.

4. Preheat the oven to 400°F (200°C). Remove the duck from the refrigerator about an hour before you plan to cook it. Roast the duck on a rack in a roasting pan in the center of the oven until the juices at the thigh run clear when pierced, about 1 hour.

5. Remove the duck from the oven and let it stand for 10 minutes. Carve, reserving some of the duck breast for the sandwiches **(see photos 01–04 on page 133)**. Arrange pieces of the duck on 4 large dinner plates. Add a Foie Gras Croissant to each plate and serve with a duck egg and small bowls of Port Wine Reduction and Red Miso Sauce for dipping.

continued . . .

Port Wine Reduction

Makes about 1 cup

Reductions are easy sauces that simply require a bit of time for the ingredients to boil down to a rich essence. If you wish, delete the Veal Reduction, but it will add body to the sauce.

2 teaspoons olive oil

1 small shallot, thinly sliced

1 small garlic clove, thinly sliced

2 cups tawny port

½ cup dry red wine

1 small sprig of fresh thyme

4 black peppercorns

1 quart (1 liter) Chicken Stock (page 256)

¼ cup Veal Reduction (page 257), or store-bought veal and duck demi-glace

1. Heat the oil in a medium saucepan over medium heat. Add the shallot and garlic and cook until the shallot softens, about 2 minutes. Add the port, red wine, thyme, and peppercorns. Bring to a boil over high heat and boil until the liquid has reduced to ½ cup.

2. Add the duck stock and boil until reduced to 1 cup, about 30 minutes. Add the Veal Reduction and cook for 5 minutes more. Strain through a sieve. Serve the reduction hot.

Foie Gras Croissants

Makes 4 croissants

Use only fresh, flaky, buttery croissants from the best bakery in town. Of course, I bake my own with foie gras, but you may not have time. You can sauté slices of fresh foie gras as directed below. Or spread smooth duck liver paté (the kind labeled "*mousse de paté*") onto the croissants.

4 best-quality buttery croissants

4 slices of fresh foie gras, cut ¼-inch (6 mm) thick (about 1 ounce/25 g each)

Salt and freshly ground white pepper

4 slices of roasted duck breast

1 scallion, cut into thin strips about 1-inch (2½ cm) long

1 Japanese or ½ seedless cucumber, thinly sliced

1. Preheat the oven to 400°F (200°C). Warm the croissants in the oven, about 5 minutes. Slice them crosswise with a serrated knife.

2. Meanwhile, heat a medium nonstick skillet over medium-high heat. Add the fresh foie gras slices and sear for 30 seconds. Turn and sear the other side until browned outside but still rare inside, about 20 seconds longer. Do not overcook the foie gras, or it will melt away.

3. Layer slices of cucumber on each croissant bottom. Add a slice of sautéed foie gras and a slice of duck breast to each. Sprinkle with the scallions and cover with the croissant tops. Serve immediately.

Chef Morimoto carves
Crispy Duck to use in two
of the three ways it is
served in his restaurants
as Duck, Duck, Duck.

Steamed Sesame Chicken

Makes 4 servings

While this recipe is labeled steamed, the chicken is actually poached, very slowly so that it remains moist and silky. This dish may start with a perfectly cooked chicken breast, which to the Japanese aesthetic is reason enough for the dish to exist. However, it is the visual effect of the opposing black and white sesame sauces that makes it extraordinary. For the juiciest chicken, give it a gentle poaching and then let it rest in the liquid to avoid overcooking it.

4 skinless, boneless chicken breasts, about 6 ounces (175 g) each

½ cup White Sesame Sauce

½ cup Black Sesame Sauce

8 teaspoons Chile Oil (page 258), as needed

1 Japanese or ½ seedless cucumber, julienned

8 cherry tomatoes, preferably 4 red and 4 yellow, halved

Fresh chives

....

WHITE SESAME SAUCE
Makes about ½ cup

¾ cup sesame seeds

½ cup Scallion Oil (page 258), as needed

1 tablespoon light-colored soy sauce

1 tablespoon sugar

2 teaspoons rice vinegar

1½ teaspoons hot sesame oil, available in Asian specialty stores

1. Bring a medium saucepan of lightly salted water to a boil over high heat. Add the chicken breasts and reduce the heat to medium-low. Cook at a steady simmer for 10 minutes. Remove the pan from the heat and cover. Let stand until the chicken looks opaque when cut in the center, about 10 minutes. Drain the chicken and let stand for 5 minutes.

2. Cut each chicken breast crosswise into ½-inch (12 mm) wide strips. Place about 1 tablespoon of White Sesame Sauce in the bottom of each of 4 wide serving bowls. Top each with a sliced breast, then drizzle with more White Sesame Sauce.

3. Using a pastry brush or the back of a soup spoon, paint swathes of the Black Sesame Sauce on the inside walls of the bowl. Drizzle a teaspoon or two over the chicken breasts along with the Chile Oil, if you like. Garnish with the cucumber, cherry tomato quarters, and chives. Serve immediately.

White Sesame Sauce

Sesame seeds can be ground into a paste then extended into a thick sauce. Regular sesame seeds make a white (actually pale gold) sauce, and black seeds, of course, a sauce of a much darker hue. You can buy sesame seeds in bulk at Asian grocers, but be sure that the regular seeds are hulled and ivory white—unhulled seeds have a grayish cast, and will make an off-white sauce.

1. Grind the sesame seeds and Scallion Oil in a blender until as smooth as possible, stopping the machine and scraping the sides of the jar as needed, about 2 minutes.

2. Add the soy sauce, sugar, rice vinegar, and hot sesame oil and blend again to combine. Adjust the consistency of the sauce with additional scallion oil. To store, cover and refrigerate for up to 1 week.

Variation: Black Sesame Sauce. Prepare the White Sesame Sauce as directed, but substitute black sesame seeds for the white ones.

LEFT: When serving soy sauce with sushi, I present them in different jars. The red one holds soy sauce for fattier fishes, the green for leaner (white-flesh) fish, and the open jar holds soy sauce for eel.

RIGHT: This plate of soy sauces represents the variety I cook with, clockwise from top left: aged soy sauce, regular (*shoyu*) soy sauce, light-colored soy sauce, and white soy sauce.

Soy Sauce

When we moved to the United States over 20 years ago, my wife and I kept many different sauces in our pantry. We had all the usual suspects, including ketchup, mayonnaise, and Worcestershire sauce. Gradually, however, our pantry full of sauces changed. Bye-bye went the Worcestershire, then the ketchup. Eventually, we even ditched the mayo. All we have left is *shoyu*, or soy sauce, and I can say with confidence that it will always be there.

The inimitable flavor of soy sauce is rich and difficult to describe. Salty, yes, but that common adjective just doesn't do it justice. Aromatic and complex, it lends a subtle muskiness, bracing sharpness, and mouthwatering tang to whatever it touches, coaxing out the sometimes shy flavors of tofu and raw fish, among other foods. Unless you use too much—its pungency can eclipse even the most powerfully flavored fish. What many people don't realize is that there is not just one soy sauce. It comes in many grades. In my restaurants, I use at least ten different varieties, each for a specific purpose, always to enhance the food it graces.

On its own, mass-produced *shoyu* is too harsh for my sushi and sashimi. The delicate flavor of raw fish and rice require something more subtle, so I temper the *shoyu* by adding some *niban dashi*—stock made from *kombu* (kelp) and *katsuobushi* (flakes of cured bonito). For the sushi and sashimi that my staff and I serve at the omakase bar, I even go a step further, buying *shoyu* with a deeper, more complex flavor from a small, family-run company in Japan. While most soy sauce is aged for less than a year, they sell *shoyu* aged from one and a half to thirty years, which vary in intensity and thickness. Each is chosen for its strength and compatibility with different foods.

At my sushi bar, I apply the perfect amount of the appropriate soy sauce to the fish in each piece of sushi before serving it to my customers. I choose to use *shoyu* of a particular age based on where the fish I'm serving came from, during what season the fish was caught, how fatty the fish is, and how the fish has been prepared. For example, I might apply a very small amount of soy sauce that has been aged for twenty years to very fatty, full-flavored cuts of fish, such as *o-toro*, which is the fattiest, most luscious part of the tuna belly. This same deep, dark sauce might overwhelm the more delicate flavor of a leaner fish. Some fish are better with a sweeter version called *nikiri-shoyu*, which is made by boiling soy sauce with sake until the alcohol is burned off. Here I distinguish even further with a darker *nikiri*, which I use with oily fish like *toro* and *hamachi* and a lighter, milder *nikiri* for white-flesh fish, shrimp, and more.

Yet another Japanese product that came from China, soy sauce entered Japan with Buddhism and the vegetarian lifestyle that came with it, eventually replacing *uoshoyu*, the fermented fish sauce that had been a popular condiment. The word soy was bestowed by Dutch merchants who brought the sauce to Europe in the 17th century; in Japan, it has long been known as *shoyu*. Now perhaps the most common Asian ingredient in the Western pantry, *shoyu* has charmed people all over the world.

Like any product, its quality varies widely, ranging from the clearly inferior to the exceptional. Mass production has generated some very weak *shoyu*, made with shortcuts and often with preservatives, while artisanal producers in Japan create intensely delicious kinds, using a combination of craft and culinary alchemy. The *shoyu*-making process begins with roasted, cracked wheat combined with soy beans that have been soaked, then steamed. A starter called *koji* (the same type of mold used in sake making) is added, which begins the process of fermentation. In one to two years, the heady brew gets mixed with a brine and left to ferment. Long ago, the mixture was aged in cedar tanks, though now most *shoyu* ferments in stainless steel. When it's ready, the liquid is filtered and pasteurized to stop the fermentation process.

All *shoyu* is broken into several types. There's *koikuchi shoyu*, the dark brown soy sauce you're used to seeing in Japanese restaurants and, probably, in your cupboard; *usukuchi shoyu*, a slightly lighter, saltier sauce used mainly for cooking (in my recipes, I call this "light-colored soy"); and tamari, a thicker sauce made without wheat. When a recipe simply calls for "soy sauce," I always mean Japanese *shoyu*. Most Chinese soy sauce has a shorter fermentation time and tastes saltier. It is best not to substitute in my recipes.

Just as home cooks add a splash to dishes that are not at all Japanese, I work both conventional dark soy and light-colored soy into many of my less-than-traditional dishes, such as Grilled Steak with Garlic-Soy Jus (see page 152) and Daikon Fettucine—my very unusual take on Italian linguine with tomato sauce (see page 170). Sometimes I blend soy and tamari for an even more complex flavor, as in my special version of Braised Black Cod (see page 114).

Angry Chicken

Makes 4 servings

2 chickens, 3½ to 4 pounds (2 kg) each, quartered

Spicy Yogurt Marinade

2 cups Chicken Stock (page 256)

24 assorted long fresh hot green and red chile peppers

2 tablespoons grape seed oil, or other vegetable oil

Fried Rice Noodles

Lime wedges, for serving

SPICY YOGURT MARINADE

Makes about 3½ cups

½ teaspoon black peppercorns

½ teaspoon cumin seeds

¼ teaspoon coriander seeds

¼ teaspoon cardamom seeds

1 teaspoon chile powder

½ teaspoon garam masala

½ teaspoon salt

1½ cups hot sauce, preferably Frank's

1⅓ cups plain yogurt

½ cup heavy cream

⅓ cup soy sauce

This is one of the most popular dishes on my menu. I have a restaurant in Mumbai, so I visit India often, and here you can see how I've been influenced by one of my favorite Indian dishes: tandoori chicken. The bird is first marinated in spiced yogurt before being roasted in a very hot oven. For garnish, I make a zesty sauce from the marinade and serve the pieces of chicken with whole grilled fresh chiles. The secret ingredient here is the hot sauce. I always use Frank's, a Louisiana-based sauce with a distinct red pepper flavor, which is neither as hot nor as sharp as other brands. As a result, the marinated chicken is certainly spicy, but not incendiary. If you want more heat, I encourage you to eat the chiles. The noodle topping is dramatic, and you'll always see it at the restaurant, but at home you can consider it optional.

1. Trim any excess fat from the chicken. Rinse and pat dry. Place the chicken quarters in a large bowl. Measure out 1 cup of the Spicy Yogurt Marinade and reserve for the sauce; refrigerate in a small covered container.

2. Pour the rest of the marinade over the chicken. Turn the pieces to make sure they are all well-coated. Cover and refrigerate for at least 8 and up to 24 hours.

3. About 1 hour before you plan to serve the chicken, preheat the oven to 450°F (230°C). Remove the chicken from the marinade and arrange the pieces on 1 or 2 half-sheet pans or large baking sheets. Discard the chicken marinade.

4. Roast for 40 minutes, until the chicken is tender and lightly browned and the juices run clear when the thighs are pricked with the tip of a small knife. Transfer the pieces to a platter and tent with foil to keep warm.

5. While the chicken is roasting, make the sauce. Boil the chicken stock in a medium saucepan over high heat until it is reduced to 1 cup. Whisk in the reserved 1 cup Spicy Yogurt Marinade and cook just until heated through; do not boil, or the yogurt will separate. Keep the sauce warm.

6. As soon as the chickens are done, preheat the broiler. Toss the chiles with the oil to coat lightly and spread them out on a broiler rack or small baking sheet. Broil the chiles about

4 inches from the heat, turning them a couple of times, until they are blistered and lightly browned, about 5 minutes.

7. To serve, layer the chicken and chiles on a large platter. Pour the sauce around the chicken. Top with the Fried Rice Noodles. Serve with lime wedges to squeeze over the chicken.

Spicy Yogurt Marinade

To make the marinade, grind the peppercorns, cumin, coriander seeds, and cardamom in a spice grinder or use a mortar and pestle. Transfer to a medium bowl. Add the chile powder, garam masala, and salt. Add the hot sauce, yogurt, cream, and soy sauce and whisk until smooth and well blended.

Fried Rice Noodles

Add vegetable oil to reach about 2 inches (5 cm) up the side of a large saucepan or a wok. Heat the oil over high heat to 340°F (170°C). Separate 1 bundle of thin rice noodles (mai fun) into 2 portions. Working with one portion at a time, add the noodles to the oil. They will puff up almost immediately. Using a large wire skimmer, transfer to paper towels to drain

Rice-Stuffed Baby Chickens

with Ginseng Root

Makes 2 to 4 servings

Baby chickens, sometimes sold by their French name, *poussins,* are tender and tasty. Stuffed with rice, the birds soak up the fragrant, ginseng- and sake-scented broth. In America, if you serve this as a main course, you may want one little chicken per person. In Japan, where we eat many small plates, we would offer half a chicken.

Note: The ginseng needs to soak for 6 hours, so begin the recipe the morning you plan to cook it or soak it overnight. The chicken, too, benefits from being salted ahead of time.

2 baby chickens (*poussins*), 12 to 16 ounces (350 to 450 g) each

Coarse salt

2 pieces of dried ginseng root, about 1-inch (2½ cm) long each

¾ cup short-grain rice

1 cup sake

1 to 1½ quarts (1 to 1½ liters) Shanton Broth or Chicken Stock (page 256)

¼ cup Chinese red raisins (*kukonomi*; also called *goji* berries)

¼ cup Chinese red dates (*natsume,* or sweetened jujubes)

Salt

1. Rinse the chickens inside and out with cold running water and pat dry. Remove the necks if they are attached; save for stock. Salt the chickens lightly, enclose in plastic wrap, and refrigerate for at least 6 and up to 24 hours.

2. At the same time, place the ginseng in a small bowl and add enough hot water to cover. Let stand until the ginseng has softened enough to slice, about 6 hours. Drain the ginseng and slice into ¼-inch (6 cm) thick rounds. There should be ¼ cup.

3. Rinse the rice. Place the rice in a medium bowl, cover with cold water, and swish the grains around a few times. Drain in a wire sieve. Repeat until the water is clear. Cover the rice with cold water and let stand for 20 to 30 minutes. Drain well.

4. Stuff the chickens with equal amounts of rice. Sew up the cavities with white kitchen string and a canvas needle, or close the cavities using small skewers. Place the trussed chickens in a saucepan or flameproof casserole just large enough to hold them in a single layer. Add the sake and enough stock to cover by about ½ inch (12 mm). Bring to a simmer over medium-high heat, skimming off the foam that rises to the surface. Add the ginseng, Chinese red raisins, and red dates. Cover and reduce the heat to medium-low. Simmer for 25 minutes.

5. Remove from the heat and let the chickens stand in the hot broth for 20 to 25 minutes longer, until the meat is white, not pink, but still juicy; an instant-read thermometer inserted in the thickest part of the breast should register 165° to 170°F (75°C). Do not let the chicken stand too long, or the meat will dry out. If serving half a chicken, transfer to a cutting board and split each chicken in half lengthwise.

6. Using a slotted spoon, transfer each chicken half to a large soup plate. Season the broth with salt to taste. Ladle some of the broth over the chickens, being sure to include the raisins and dates, but discard the ginseng. (Save the extra broth, if you like, for another meal.)

Chicken Sukiyaki

Makes 4 servings

8 ounces (225 g) firm tofu

1 package (7 ounces/200 g) yam noodles *(shirataki)*, drained and rinsed, or substitute three-bean thread noodles

4 cups **Dashi** (page 256)

½ cup mirin

½ cup sake

⅓ cup soy sauce

12 ounces (350 g) skinless, boneless chicken breast, cut into chunks

2 cups cut-up Napa cabbage, 1-inch (2½ cm) pieces

12 fresh shiitake mushrooms, stemmed and wiped clean

2 packed cups chrysanthemum leaves, or stemmed watercress, or spinach leaves

1 Tokyo scallion, white part only, sliced

1 bunch of enoki mushrooms, trimmed and sliced in half crosswise

Sukiyaki is one of those communal dishes where the pot is brought to the table and everyone gets to participate, dipping in and pulling out each favorite ingredient as it is cooked.

1. Preheat a stovetop grill pan. Lightly oil the pan. Slice the tofu in half horizontally. Grill the tofu, turning once, until seared with grill marks on both sides, about 2 minutes per side. Cut the pieces into bite-size cubes.

2. Bring a medium saucepan of water to a boil over high heat. Add the *shirataki* and reduce the heat to low. Simmer for 1 minute to refresh the noodles, then drain and rinse under cold running water. Set aside.

3. Choose a pot, preferably ceramic, that can go from the stove to the table. Or use a chafing dish. Pour the Dashi, mirin, sake, and soy sauce into the pot and bring to a boil over high heat. Add the chicken, cabbage, and mushrooms and return the liquid to a boil. Add the reserved yam noodles

4. Transfer the pot to a hot plate or candle flame on the table and adjust the heat to keep the broth at a gentle simmer. Add the chrysanthemum leaves, scallion, and enoki mushrooms. Each diner uses chopsticks to retrieve the ingredients from the broth as they are cooked.

Grilled Quail Morimoto-Style

Makes 4 servings

Because these tasty birds are so small, you'll want to serve them as an appetizer. Otherwise, allow two per person. If the quail are not semiboneless, ask the butcher to prepare them for you. Or bone them yourself as follows: Split each bird down either side of the backbone; remove the bone. Slip a small sharp knife between the breast meat and the ribs and work it, scraping the breast meat off the ribs. Save the backbone and rib bones for stock.

4 semiboneless quail, butterflied

1 tablespoon vegetable oil

1 cup Teriyaki Jus

1 tablespoon chopped _kinome_, or fresh mint

....

TERIYAKI JUS

Makes about 1 cup

½ cup unsalted chicken broth

⅓ cup sake

⅓ cup soy sauce

⅓ cup mirin

⅓ cup sugar

2 teaspoons cornstarch, dissolved in 1 tablespoon water

1. Insert 4 metal skewers or 4 bamboo skewers soaked in water crosswise into each quail to keep the birds from curling when cooked.

2. Prepare a hot fire in an outdoor grill or preheat the broiler. Lightly brush each quail with vegetable oil. Grill skin side toward the fire to sear lightly, 1 to 2 minutes. Turn over and sear the second side for 1 to 2 minutes.

3. Brush the skin side with Teriyaki Jus and turn over. Brush the inside of the bird with Teriyaki Jus and cook for 30 seconds before turning again. Continue basting and turning until the quail are glazed, browned, and tender, about 3 minutes. The breast meat is best medium-rare.

4. Serve immediately, garnished with the _kinome_ or mint.

Teriyaki Jus

1. Put the chicken broth in a small saucepan and boil until reduced by half, 3 to 5 minutes.

2. Add in the sake, soy sauce, mirin, and sugar. Bring to a boil, stirring to dissolve the sugar. Then simmer until the sauce is reduced to 1 cup, about 8 to 10 minutes.

3. Stir in the cornstarch and bring to a boil, stirring until thickened and smooth. The sauce can be made up to 5 days in advance. Let cool, then refrigerate in a covered container.

Grilled Pork Chops

with Enoki Mushrooms, Napa Cabbage, and Tonkotsu Broth

Makes 4 servings

Pork chops are a favorite Japanese cut. I present them in a bowl of savory broth made from pork bones and *kombu*, the same seaweed used in Dashi. While here the meat is shown with cabbage, mushrooms, and peas, you can choose the vegetable garnish of your choice.

4 (8-ounce/225-g) pork loin chops, bone-in, about 1-inch (2½ cm) thick

¼ cup extra virgin olive oil

Salt and freshly ground black pepper

2 teaspoons unsalted butter

½ pound (225 g) Napa cabbage, shredded

1 bunch of enoki mushrooms, trimmed and sliced in half crosswise

1 bunch of scallions, cut into 1-inch (2½ cm) lengths

2 cups Tonkotsu Broth

4 teaspoons peas

Sprigs of *kinome*, for garnish

·····································

TONKOTSU BROTH
Makes about 2 cups

¾ pound (350 g) pork neck bones, or pork shanks

¾ pound (350 g) pork spareribs

3-inch (7 cm) piece of *kombu*

1 teaspoon salt

1 tablespoon sake

1 tablespoon light-colored soy sauce

1. Prepare a hot fire in an outdoor grill or heat a heavy grill pan over medium-high heat. Brush the pork chops lightly with olive oil and season with salt and pepper. Grill the chops, for 3 to 4 minutes, rotating about halfway through, to form nice brown grill marks. Turn the chops off and grill until the chops are browned on the second side and the meat is no longer pink in the center, about 3 to 4 minutes longer. Set aside on a plate and cover to keep warm while you prepare the cabbage.

2. In a sauté pan or large skillet, melt the butter in the remaining olive oil over medium-high heat. Add the cabbage, mushrooms, and scallions and sauté until the cabbage softens, about 3 minutes. Season with salt and pepper to taste.

3. To serve, mound the cabbage and mushrooms in the center of 4 large soup bowls. Add a pork chop to each bowl and ladle the Tonkotsu Broth over all. Add the peas and *kinome* for garnish.

Tonkotsu Broth

1. In a large pot of boiling water, blanch the pork neck bones and spareribs for 3 to 5 minutes. Drain, then plunge the bones into cold water to remove extra surface fat and residue. Rinse out the pot.

2. Add 6 cups fresh water, the kombu, and the blanched pork and bones to the pot. Bring to a boil, skimming off any scum that rises to the top. When the liquid is clear, cover, reduce the heat to low, and simmer for 3 hours. Strain and let cool, then cover and refrigerate. The fat can be scraped right off the top.

3. Add the salt, sake, and soy sauce to the Tonkotsu Broth before adding it to the Pork Chops.

Pork Kakuni

Makes 4 servings

Everyone loves my Pork Kakuni, slow-braised pork belly that literally melts in the mouth. This is a healthy dish in that most of the fat is gone by the time the pork is fully cooked. I serve it as an appetizer atop the porridgelike Scallop Congee.

Note that the brown rice in the initial long, slow braising acts as a tenderizer, so that the final product is soft enough to eat with a spoon; white rice cannot be substituted. Even the tough pork rind becomes meltingly tender. The longer you make this ahead, the better. If you're serving it on the weekend, begin preparations on Thursday.

1 tablespoon vegetable oil

2 pounds (900 g) boneless pork belly, in one piece

1½ cups brown rice

1¾ cups sake

¼ cup soy sauce

2 tablespoons sugar

Scallop Congee (recipe follows)

Crispy Burdock (page 260) and minced scallions, for garnish

1. Preheat the oven to 250°F (120°C). Heat the oil in a large flameproof casserole just big enough to hold the pork over medium-high heat. Add the pork belly, skin side down, and sear until golden brown, about 5 minutes. Turn over and brown on the other side, about 5 minutes longer. Transfer to a plate. Pour off the fat in the casserole.

2. Return the pork belly to the casserole. Sprinkle the brown rice over the meat. Pour in enough cold water to cover by an inch and bring to a simmer over high heat. Cover with the lid and transfer to the oven. Braise gently until the pork is tender when pierced with a knife, about 8 hours. Do not overcook at this point, keeping in mind that the meat will cook for 2 hours longer later. Remove from the oven, uncover, and let the pork cool for a couple of hours in the cooking liquid.

3. Carefully remove the pork from the liquid, keeping it in one piece. Discard the rice and cooking liquid. Cover and refrigerate the pork belly for at least 8 hours, or up to 2 days.

4. Cut the pork crosswise into 4 pieces about 2½-inches (6 cm) wide. In a heavy medium saucepan, mix the sake, soy sauce, and sugar with 4 cups of water and bring to a boil over high heat, stirring to dissolve the sugar. Add the pork belly and reduce the heat to low. Partially cover the pan and simmer until the pork is very tender, about 2 hours.

5. Using a wide slotted spatula, carefully transfer the pork belly to a plate, taking care that it doesn't fall apart, and cover with foil to keep warm. Strain the cooking liquid into a large skillet and quickly boil over high heat until it is reduced to 1 cup, about 10 minutes.

6. To serve, spoon equal amounts of the Scallop Congee into 4 bowls. Top each with a piece of pork and about 2 tablespoons of the reduced sauce. Garnish with the Crispy Burdock and minced scallions. Serve immediately.

continued . . .

146

Scallop Congee

Makes 4 servings

Congee, which is rice porridge, is a popular breakfast meal in China. Here, seasoned with dried scallops, it serves as a bed for long-simmered pork. Before cooking, allow time for the rice to stand overnight and become infused with the Scallion Oil.

¼ cup short-grain rice

2 tablespoons Scallion Oil (page 258)

2 dried scallops

1¾ cups Chicken Stock (page 256)

Sea salt

1. Rinse the rice in a mesh sieve placed inside a bowl of cold water. Swish it around, lift the sieve and change the water. Repeat until the water runs clear. Drain well.

2. Transfer the rice to a small bowl, add the Scallion Oil and toss to mix well. Cover with plastic wrap and let the rice stand at room temperature for at least 8 hours or overnight.

3. Soak the scallops in warm water to cover for 20 minutes. Drain the scallops and flake them into small pieces.

4. Combine the oil-coated rice, flaked scallops, Chicken Stock, and 1¾ cups water in a heavy medium saucepan. Bring to a boil over high heat, stirring often. Reduce the heat to medium-low. Cook at a brisk simmer, uncovered, stirring often, until the rice has broken down into porridge, about 45 minutes. Season with salt to taste and serve hot.

Japanese Knives and
Other Special Equipment

Decades ago, almost every Japanese kitchen had a *katsuobushi kezuri*, a wooden box outfitted with a blade on one side. When cooks wanted to make *dashi*, the quick stock used in countless Japanese dishes, they would take a block of *katsuobushi* (dried, smoked, cured bonito that's as hard as wood) and run it again and again against the blade. The wispy flakes of fish, needed to make the stock, collected in the box. Since their flavor and aroma degrade soon after shaving, doing this makes for better dashi. We used to use a *katsuobushi kezuri* at my restaurants, but I recently found a machine that allows us to quickly shave the large amount of *katsuobushi* that we need for service. It's more efficient and does not sacrifice quality.

This balance of quality and efficiency in the kitchen is essential. Both Western and Japanese kitchens have changed dramatically over the years—in some ways for the better, in some for the worse. What I strive for in my kitchen is a mix of old and new that at once embraces tradition and innovation. For instance, when a dish warrants it, I love introducing my customers to fresh wasabi. I often grate the fresh, green rhizome shortly before serving it, and the best way to do that has traditionally been, and still is, by using a sharkskin grater. Graters with metal teeth work well for *daikon* and *yamanoimo*, or mountain yam, but the sharkskin, naturally coated with tiny bumps, provides the ideal roughness to give the wasabi the proper texture and to coax out its distinctive sweet, spicy taste. When it's chopped, sliced, or shredded, its flavor remains quiet. Only when grated to a fine paste does wasabi's full flavor and powerful pungency reveal itself.

You won't find many of my most prized pieces of equipment in other professional kitchens. Take my rice mill, a square four-foot-tall machine used for hulling rice. Every day, my chefs pass *genmai*, or brown rice, through the

ABOVE: **When the *sakimaru takobiki* knife on the left was made for me, it was the longest knife ever made of that type, used for sashimi.**

RIGHT: **These special pieces of equipment include the dried bonito shaver (*katsuobushi kezuri*) and the sharkskin grater for fresh wasabi root.**

149

LEFT: **You can tell that these *yanagi-ba* knives age from left to right—the oldest is most worn away at the handle from use and daily cleaning and at the blade from sharpening.**

RIGHT: **At left are *mori-bashi*, steel chopsticks made especially for plating. The handles are made from tortoise-shell. These two *deba-bocho* knives and *yanagi-ba* knife (at right) are the ones I used for all my "Iron Chef" battles. Their handles are made from deer antlers.**

FAR RIGHT: **This rare sharpening stone is made from one piece of stone taken from the mountains in Kyoto, Japan.**

mill. Seconds later, it spits out little pearly white grains. The brown rice, which has its husk intact, remains fresher with moisture and flavor much longer than unprotected white rice, which is why I begin with the whole grain. Each morning we decide how much rice we need, and we process just enough for that day. The machine lets me decide exactly how far to polish. I always leave a little of the outside for flavor and texture and make sure to preserve the entire *haiga*, or rice germ, which is nutritious and slightly sweet.

I'm willing to bet you wouldn't find my special tuna freezer in other kitchens either. I like to call it a "super freezer," since it has the capacity to cool to minus 86°C. The super freezer ensures that the pricey fish freezes quickly and maintains its high quality. Why do I freeze my tuna? Because it allows me to serve the best tuna, which I can only buy in season.

Perhaps the most personal tools in my kitchen are my knives. This is partly because I use knives that have been custom made for me. They are the ideal thickness, length, and heaviness for the way I work. For instance, while some knives must be heavy enough to break through bones, when forged by a skilled craftsman, the weight is meticulously distributed, so that the chef hardly feels the heft. I feel very close to these knives because in the kitchen they act as an extension of my arm, just as I expect golf clubs do for Tiger Woods. I have a lot of practice slicing fish, so when I cut, I do so almost instinctively, knowing exactly what I want to accomplish with each stroke. Without a knife that you have complete control of, there is a disconnect between arm and action. The result is not perfect, and that's unacceptable.

To do the dirty work—gutting and filleting fish—I use a knife with a thick, triangular blade called *deba-bocho*, which comes in various sizes and degrees of thickness, depending upon its specific purpose. For slicing fish

for sashimi and *sushi*, I use several long, elegant-looking knives of various lengths called *yanagi-ba*. These are unbelievably sharp, like razors. The better the knife, the more care it takes to properly sharpen it and to produce clean, precise cuts. This also allows you to make long, sliding incisions that don't rupture the cells of the fish, which can ruin its texture and taste. There are even knives with exceptionally thin blades used specifically for cutting *fugu* (blowfish) into thin, translucent slices, a technique known as *usuzukuri*. The blade of a *yanagi-ba* is usually up to a foot long, though for special purposes, there is even one that is twice that length.

If you're thinking that this sounds more like a weapon than a kitchen knife, then you're on to something. In the Edo Period, a time of relative peace in Japan, some sword makers turned their skills toward making knives. During the Meiji Restoration in the 1860s, the government banned samurai from wearing their swords, so many more artisans devoted themselves completely to this culinary tool. And I'm glad they did. They brought the great care that went into crafting an implement meant to ensure one's survival to one built for another essential purpose.

Yet a great knife does not make a great chef. Some chefs buy fine, expensive knives just because they think they look cool, but they can't use them correctly. They are missing the point. Yes, you need a sharp knife, but a sharp arm—and eye—is even more important.

Duck, Chicken, Pork, Beef, and Lamb

Grilled Steak with Garlic-Soy Jus

Makes 4 servings

When serving steak at home, you can get that tasty browned crust that is the goal of every chef. The secret is a very, very hot cast-iron skillet. At my restaurants, I instruct my chefs to heat the pan for a full 20 minutes. Your kitchen smoke alarm may disagree, but heat it as long as you can. For four servings, you will need two large cast-iron skillets, as you do not want to crowd the steaks, or they will steam and not brown. Grapeseed oil is used because it has the highest smoking point of any cooking oil, but the dish is finished with a basting of butter.

4 boneless strip or rib-eye steaks, preferably Kobe or Wagyu, cut about ¾-inch (2 cm) thick

Salt and freshly ground black pepper

2 tablespoons grape seed oil, or olive oil

6 tablespoons unsalted butter, cut up

Garlic-Soy Jus

....

GARLIC-SOY JUS

Makes about 1 cup

6 garlic cloves, chopped

3 tablespoons chopped, peeled fresh ginger

2 tablespoons sugar

½ cup Veal Reduction (page 257)

½ cup soy sauce

½ cup mirin

2 teaspoons sesame oil

1 small onion, peeled

1. Heat two large cast-iron skillets over high heat for at least 5 and preferably 10 minutes, until they are extremely hot. While the pans are heating, season the steaks with salt and pepper to taste.

2. Pour 1 tablespoon of the oil into each skillet and tilt the pans to coat the bottoms lightly. Immediately place 2 steaks in each skillet. Cook over high heat until the undersides are well browned, 2 to 2½ minutes. Turn and brown the other sides, about 2 to 2½ minutes longer.

3. Reduce the heat to medium-low. Attending to one skillet at a time, add 3 tablespoons butter and spoon it over the meat as it melts. The butter should turn dark brown, but not black. Do this quickly and continue to cook the steaks until they are rare, about 1½ minutes longer; the meat will feel soft like a ripe peach when pressed. Remove from the heat and let stand for 10 minutes.

4. Transfer the steaks to a platter and pour the browned butter over them. Serve the steaks with a tablespoon or two of Garlic-Soy Jus drizzled over the top. Pass the remaining sauce on the side.

Garlic-Soy Jus

The consistency of this *jus* may be thin, but it is pleasantly heavy with the bold flavors of garlic and ginger. Use it with steaks or chops, or to moisten Buri Bop (see page 54).

1. Mix the garlic and ginger together on a cutting board and chop them until minced. Sprinkle them with about 1½ teaspoons of the sugar, and continue chopping and smearing with the flat side of the knife until they form a paste. Transfer to a bowl.

2. Mix in the Veal Reduction, soy sauce, mirin, sesame oil, and the remaining sugar, stirring to dissolve the sugar. Grate the onion into the hot liquid.

3. Let the sauce stand for 1 hour to blend the flavors. If not used at once, store the *jus* in a covered container in the refrigerator for up to 1 week. Reheat before using.

Miso-Braised Short Ribs Tempura

Makes 4 servings

8 meaty short ribs on the bone, cut 3 to 4 inches (8 cm) long (about 3 pounds/1¼ kg)

1 teaspoon white peppercorns

1 teaspoon black peppercorns

1 teaspoon Sichuan peppercorns

2 bay leaves

2 sprigs of fresh thyme, or ½ teaspoon dried

2 quarts Shanton Broth (page 256)

¼ cup red miso

Vegetable oil, for deep-frying

1 cup all-purpose flour

Small-Batch Tempura Batter

....

SMALL-BATCH
TEMPURA BATTER
Makes about 1½ cups

1 egg yolk

¼ cup vegetable oil

¾ cup chilled club soda

1 cup all-purpose flour

These morsels juxtapose tender, juicy beef with a crispy tempura crust. The short ribs go through a two-step braising, first in a spiced broth to remove excess fat, then in a miso-flavored stock, which intensifies the taste. Finally, the bones are removed, and the silky meat is coated in tempura batter and fried until crisp.

A few notes: It is important to buy meaty short ribs on the bone that have been cut into 3- to 4-inch (8 cm) lengths; don't confuse these with cross-cut ribs, which are also called flanken. The meat will shrink quite a bit during braising, so if you start off with skimpy ribs, you won't have anything left for the tempura. This recipe can be prepared a day in advance through step 3, which will make last-minute preparations much simpler.

1. Trim off any excess fat from the short ribs. In a large saucepan or flameproof casserole, combine 3 quarts (3 liters) of water, the black, white, and Sichuan peppercorns, bay leaves, and thyme. Bring to a boil over high heat. Add the short ribs and partially cover the pot. Reduce the heat to low. Simmer the ribs, skimming off any foam from the surface, until the meat is almost tender when pierced with the tip of a sharp knife, about 1½ hours. Do not overcook, because the ribs will cook further in two later steps. Remove the ribs from the braising liquid and let cool to room temperature.

2. Bring the Shanton Broth and red miso to a boil in the large saucepan over high heat, whisking to dissolve the miso. Add the short ribs and reduce the heat to low. Simmer, uncovered, turning occasionally, until the ribs are very tender but not falling apart, about 1½ hours. Using a slotted spoon, transfer the short ribs to a plate and let cool completely. Then remove the meat from the bones, trying to keep each rib in one chunk.

3. While the ribs are cooling, skim off as much fat as you can from the Shanton-miso broth. Boil over high heat until the liquid is reduced to 1 cup, about 20 minutes. Strain the sauce and set aside. (The short ribs and sauce can be

prepared up to 1 day ahead, separately cooled, covered, and refrigerated. Remove the short ribs from the refrigerator at least 1 hour before deep-frying.)

4. Preheat the oven to 200°F (90°C). Heat the oil in a deep fryer or pour vegetable oil into a large saucepan to reach halfway up the sides. Heat over high heat to 350°F (180°C).

5. Working with half of the short ribs at a time, coat the ribs with the all-purpose flour, shaking off any excess. Dip in the tempura batter and let extra batter drip back into the bowl. Add the coated ribs to the hot oil and deep-fry until light golden brown, about 2 minutes. Using a slotted skimmer, transfer to a wire rack set on a baking sheet to drain. Keep warm in the low oven while frying the remaining short ribs.

6. To serve, spoon equal amounts of the sauce onto 4 dinner plates. Top each with 2 pieces of Short Rib Tempura and serve immediately.

Small-Batch Tempura Batter

In a medium bowl, beat the egg yolk with a fork. Whisk in the vegetable oil until blended and then the club soda. Add the flour and stir with chopsticks until just barely combined. Don't worry if some flour floats on top.

Nikujaga

Makes 4 servings

Americans do not have a corner on the concept of meat and potatoes for dinner. Although neither meat (*niku*) nor potatoes (*jagaimo*) are traditional Japanese ingredients, *Nikujaga* is typical of Japanese home cooking. Like other dishes I have expanded on, I've enjoyed transforming this humble stew into an elegant dish.

2 quarts Beef Stock
(page 257)

1 cup mirin

1 cup Japanese soy sauce

1 cup sugar

4 small potatoes, peeled and cut into 1-inch (2½ cm) pieces

3 narrow carrots, cut into 1-inch (2½ cm) lengths

2 medium onions, cut into 1-inch (2½ cm) pieces

1 cup haricots verts or narrow green beans, trimmed

8 ounces (225 g) yam noodles (*shirataki*), rinsed and drained, snipped with scissors into 5-inch (12½ cm) lengths

1¼ pounds (575 g) thinly sliced top loin, preferably prime, Kobe, or Wagyu

Zest of 1 *yuzu*, or lemon, for garnish

1. Bring 1 quart (1 liter) beef stock, ½ cup mirin, ½ cup soy sauce, and ½ cup sugar to a boil in a large deep skillet over high heat, stirring to dissolve the sugar. Add the potatoes, carrots, and onions, adding a little more stock or water to cover the vegetables, if needed. Reduce the heat to moderately low and cover. Simmer until the vegetables are just tender, about 30 minutes. Set aside.

2. Bring the remaining 1 quart (1 liter) beef stock, ½ cup mirin, ½ cup soy sauce, and ½ cup sugar to a boil in a large saucepan over high heat, stirring to dissolve the sugar. Reduce the heat to medium-low, bringing the stock to a bare simmer.

3. Blanch the green beans in a medium saucepan of lightly salted water over high heat until crisp-tender, about 30 seconds. Drain, rinse briefly under running water, and drain again well.

4. Meanwhile, return the previously cooked potatoes, carrots, and onions with their liquid to a simmer. Add the yam noodles and cook until the vegetables are heated through. Divide the vegetables and broth among 4 bowls.

5. Using chopsticks or tongs, dip the meat into the simmering stock and heat just until the meat begins to change color; it should remain very rare and only takes a few seconds for each slice. As it is cooked, drape the sliced meat over the vegetables.

6. In a separate pan, pour in 3 cups of the remaining stock and reduce it over medium heat to 1 cup, about 30 minutes. Pour the reduced liquid over the meat and vegetables, top with the green beans, garnish with the *yuzu* zest, and serve immediately.

Hayashi Stew

Makes 4 servings

1 tablespoon vegetable oil

1 large onion, sliced

6 tablespoons unsalted butter

1½ pounds (675 g) Wagyu
or other top-quality boneless
beef chuck, cut against the
grain into slices about 1½-
inches (4 cm) long and ½-inch
(1 cm) thick

1 garlic clove, chopped

1 cup hearty red wine

3 tablespoons tomato ketchup

2 cups Veal Stock
(page 257)

2 cups Shanton Broth or
Chicken Stock (page 256)

¼ cup all-purpose flour

Salt and freshly ground
black pepper

Hayashi Stew is another popular Japanese dish that I have enjoyed refining. It is a Western-style dish, similar to boeuf Bourguignon, with lots of body and depth of flavor. Serve with steamed white rice.

1. Heat the oil in a large flameproof casserole or Dutch oven over medium-high heat. Add the onion and sauté, stirring often, until the slices are golden brown, 5 to 7 minutes. Remove the onions to a plate.

2. Melt 3 tablespoons of the butter in the same casserole, add the meat and garlic, and cook, turning the slices occasionally, until they are no longer pink, 3 to 5 minutes. Set aside on the plate with the onions. Pour the red wine into the pot and bring to a boil, scraping up the browned bits with a wooden spatula.

3. Blend in the ketchup and return the beef and onions to the casserole. Pour in the Veal Stock and the Shanton Broth and bring to a simmer. Reduce the heat to medium-low, cover, and simmer until the meat is almost tender, about 1½ hours.

4. Melt the remaining 3 tablespoons of butter in a heavy medium saucepan over medium heat. Whisk in the flour and cook, stirring, for 2 to 3 minutes. Gradually ladle in about 2 cups of the hot stew cooking liquid and bring to a boil, whisking until thickened and smooth.

5. Stir the thickened liquid back into the stew. Continue to simmer, covered, until the meat is very tender, about 30 minutes. Season with salt and pepper to taste.

Beef Cutlet Sandwich

Makes 4 servings

Fried breaded pork cutlet, called *tonkatsu*, is a common Japanese lunch dish, but I use top-quality beef. I sandwich the meat between slices of toasted bread. *Tonkatsu* is always served with a tangy sauce, which can be purchased in bottles at Asian specialty stores. At the restaurant, we serve this sandwich with fried sweet onion rings and pickles.

12 ounces (350 g) Wagyu or other top-quality tri-tip or fillet of beef, cut into 4 slices about ½-inch (1 cm) thick (see Note)

Salt and freshly ground black pepper

2 tablespoons unsalted butter, softened

1 tablespoon Dijon mustard

1 cup all-purpose flour

2 large eggs, beaten

1 cup Japanese bread crumbs (panko)

Vegetable oil, for frying

8 thick slices of firm white sandwich bread, lightly toasted

3 tablespoons mayonnaise

¾ cup very thinly shredded green cabbage

⅓ cup *tonkatsu* sauce, available in Asian specialty stores

1. Using a flat meat mallet, gently pound the meat until the slices are about ½-inch (1 cm) thick and just a little smaller than the bread slices. Season on both sides with salt and pepper to taste.

2. Mix the butter and mustard in a small bowl and blend well. Set the mustard butter aside at room temperature.

3. Put the flour, beaten eggs, and *panko* in 3 separate shallow dishes. One by one, dredge the beef slices in flour to coat on both sides; shake off any excess. Dip the cutlets in the eggs, then press into the bread crumbs to coat both sides.

4. Pour ½ inch (1 cm) of oil into a large skillet and set over high heat until the oil shimmers. Add the cutlets to the hot oil and fry quickly, turning once, until golden brown and crisp on both sides and still rare in the center, about 3 minutes total. Drain on paper towels.

5. Quickly spread the mustard butter over one side of 4 slices of bread, and the mayonnaise over the remaining 4 slices. Set a cutlet on each mustard-butter coated bread slice. Top with about 3 tablespoons shredded cabbage and 1 to 1½ tablespoons *tonkatsu* sauce. Cap the sandwiches with the remaining bread slices. Cut each in half and serve immediately.

Note: We always use Wagyu tri-tip beef at my restaurants, but that cut of meat is not easily available at retail. If you have a cooperative butcher, you might be able to get prime grade tri-tip, but choice is acceptable, too. Buy a typical tri-tip roast, which weighs about 1½ pounds (675 g). Cut the meat at a slight diagonal across the grain to get 4 wide, ½-inch (1 cm) thick slices. If using prime or choice beef fillet, have the butcher cut it, or select 2 center-cut filet mignon steaks, weighing about 6 ounces (175 g) each. Then cut each steak horizontally in half.

Lamb Carpaccio

Makes 4 servings

Slicing the lamb thin is a crucial element in this dish. Freezing the meat for about 1 hour will make it firmer and much easier to slice thinly. Needless to say, let your butcher know you are planning to serve the meat raw.*

½ pound (225 g) boneless lamb loin, or tenderloin

Sea salt and coarsely cracked black peppercorns

2 teaspoons fresh lemon juice

2 tablespoons Scallion-Ginger Sauce

3 chives, preferably Japanese baby chives (menegi) cut into 1-inch (2½ cm) pieces, for garnish

3 shiso buds, or garlic flowers, for garnish

....

SCALLION-GINGER SAUCE

Makes about ½ cup

1 small scallion (white and green parts), finely minced

2 tablespoons finely minced peeled fresh ginger

¼ cup vegetable oil

1 teaspoon finely chopped pickled wasabi root with leaves, optional

1. Slice the lamb against the grain into very thin slices and season with a large pinch of sea salt and freshly cracked black peppercorns to taste. Drizzle the lemon juice over the meat and roll up.

2. Arrange the lamb on a platter or individual plates. Top each roll with about ¼ teaspoon of the Scallion-Ginger Sauce. Garnish the platter with the chive pieces and *shiso* buds. Serve at once.

Scallion-Ginger Sauce

1. This recipe yields more than you will need for the Lamb Carpaccio. The richly flavored oil keeps quite well in the refrigerator for up to 5 days and is a wonderful sauce for drizzling over steamed or fried dumplings, grilled fish, or steak. **Note: The oil is not drained before use; both the oil and the minced aromatics are served together as a sauce.**

2. Place the minced scallion and ginger along the bottom of a heatproof bowl. Heat the oil in a small saucepan until quite hot. Carefully pour the hot oil over the scallion and ginger. Cool briefly, then stir in the wasabi root. Let the sauce sit for at least 1 hour before using.

*Editor's Note: Raw lamb is not appropriate for pregnant women or people with an impaired immune system.

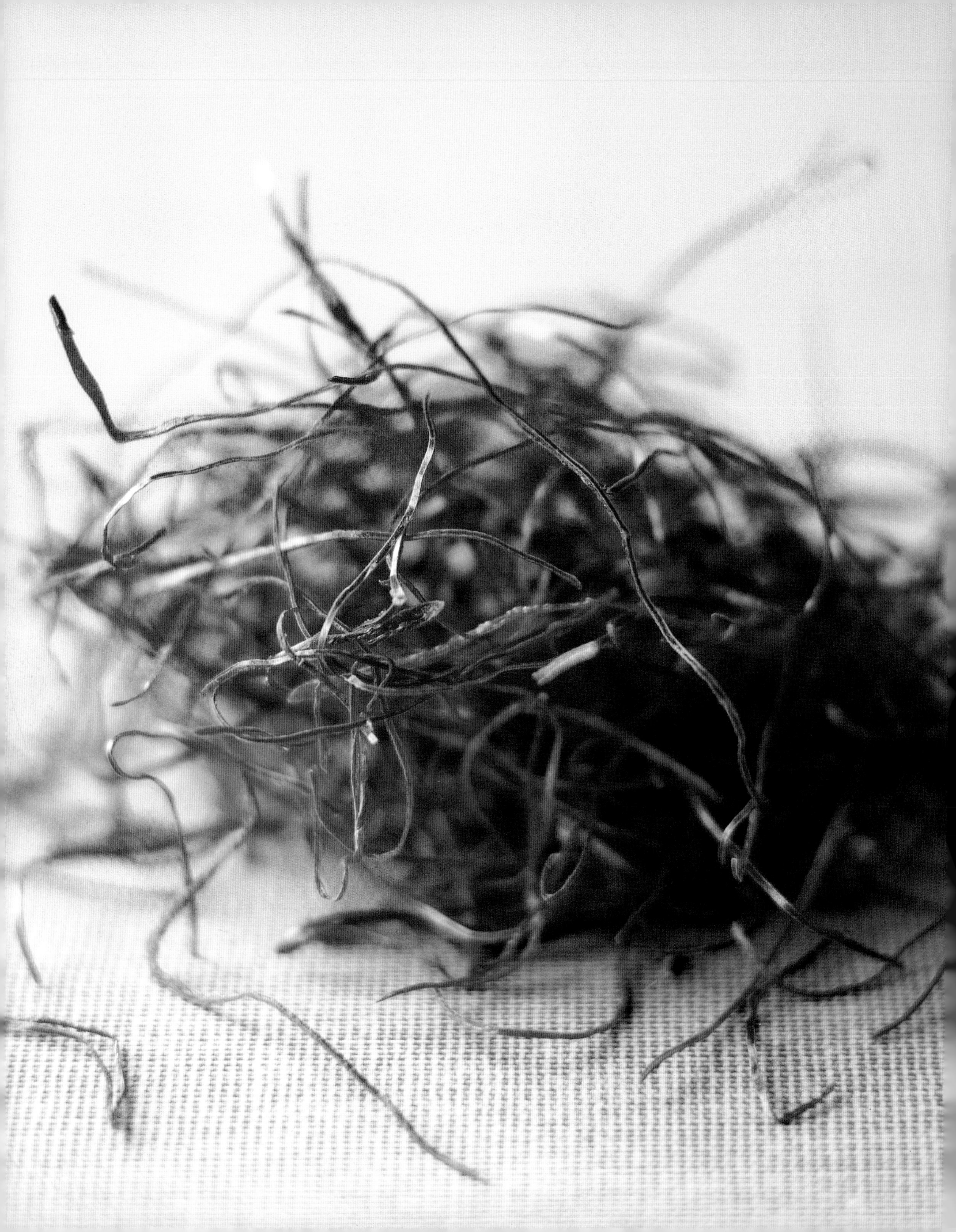

Vegetables, Tofu, and Eggs

Asparagus Salad

with Fresh Tomato and Shiso Dressing

Makes 4 servings

Simple and colorful, this salad works well either as a light starter or as a refresher after the main course. Since the raw asparagus must be prepared ahead of time, it is an excellent dish for home entertaining. To preserve the lovely flavor of *shiso*'s volatile oils, make the dressing at the last minute.

Note: While we like to present a duo of different colored asparagus, as shown in the photograph, you can make this with all white or all green asparagus. garnish it with shaved dried bonito and *arasumi*.

6 green asparagus spears

6 white asparagus spears

2 small vine-ripe tomatoes or large plum tomatoes, peeled, seeded, and coarsely chopped (about 4 ounces/100 g)

2 large *shiso* leaves, torn up

½ cup extra virgin olive oil

Salt and freshly ground black pepper

Juice of 1 *sudachi,* or key lime

1. Trim off the bottoms of the asparagus stems. With the tip of a small knife, grasp a strip of asparagus skin at the bottom and pull up to remove. If it doesn't come off easily, peel with a swivel-blade vegetable peeler. Continue to run the peeler down the length of the peeled asparagus stalks to cut them into very thin strips, or ribbons, setting aside the green and white separately. Soak the asparagus strips in 2 bowls of ice water for 5 to 10 minutes to crisp.

2. To make the Tomato and Shiso Dressing: Purée the tomatoes and *shiso* in a food processor or blender. With the machine on, slowly add the olive oil. Season with salt and pepper to taste. Spoon about 1 tablespoon of the Tomato and Shiso Dressing onto each of 4 plates.

3. Drain the asparagus strips and pat dry on a kitchen towel. Pile the asparagus on top of the sauce in 2 mounds. Drizzle another tablespoon of dressing over the asparagus and sprinkle the *sudachi* or lime juice. Serve immediately.

Bamboo Shoots with Fresh Mint

Makes 4 servings

As with many of my dishes, this is a small salad, which you'll want to serve with something else. The bright green herbal sauce, a blend of fresh mint and spinach mixed with my White Miso Sauce, makes a pretty contrast to the yellow bamboo shoots. This is a very typical Spring dish in Japan, usually served with *kinome* leaves. As they are not easily available in the United States, I decided to use the fresh mint, which you can get in any supermarket.

2 small bamboo shoots, canned

2 cups Dashi (page 256)

1 tablespoon mirin

1 teaspoon light-colored soy sauce

Salt

¼ cup fresh spinach leaves

2 tablespoons fresh mint leaves, plus small sprigs for garnish

½ cup White Miso Sauce (page 259)

½ teaspoon sesame seeds

1. Rinse each bamboo shoot and cut into 4 pieces. In a medium saucepan, combine the Dashi, mirin, and soy sauce. Season lightly with salt to taste. Bring to a simmer, add the bamboo shoots, and cook until they are tender, about 5 minutes. Remove the pan from the heat and let the bamboo shoots cool in the cooking liquid for 30 to 40 minutes.

2. Meanwhile, in a saucepan of boiling water, blanch the spinach and mint until wilted but still bright green, about 30 seconds. Drain and rinse under cold running water; squeeze dry. Purée in a blender or mini food processor.

3. Transfer the spinach-mint purée to a bowl. Mix in the White Miso Sauce. Add the bamboo shoots and stir to coat. Serve, garnished with the sesame seeds and springs of mint.

Daikon Fettucine with Tomato-Basil Sauce

Makes 3 to 4 servings

By now, you've probably figured out I am very fond of visual puns. Here ribbons of *daikon*, the mild oversized white Japanese radish, pose as pasta. They are tossed with a quick tomato sauce spiked with a generous amount of fresh basil. The dish is light and is best served as a first course.

1 pound (450 g) daikon

1 can (14½ ounces/400 g) plum tomatoes

3 tablespoons extra virgin olive oil

1 small onion, finely chopped

2 garlic cloves, minced

1½ to 2 teaspoons sugar

1 teaspoon salt

1 tablespoon chopped fresh basil

Salt and freshly ground black pepper

1. With a swivel-blade vegetable peeler, remove the outer skin of the daikon **(photo 01)**; discard the skin. Continue to peel down the length of the vegetable, removing the daikon in long, narrow ribbons, which look like noodles **(photos 02 and 03)**. Soak the "fettuccine" in a bowl of cold salted water for 15 to 20 minutes **(photo 04)**.

2. Meanwhile, make the Tomato-Basil Sauce: Drain the tomatoes, reserving half of the juice. Squeeze the tomatoes through your fingers to mash them and combine with the juice; there will be about 2 cups.

3. In a heavy medium saucepan, heat the oil over medium-high heat. Add the onion and garlic and sauté until softened but not browned, about 3 minutes. Add the tomatoes and their reserved juice, the sugar, and the salt. Boil vigorously,

stirring often, until the sauce is thick, 10 to 15 minutes. Stir in the basil and season with salt and pepper to taste.

4. Drain the "noodles" and dry them on a kitchen towel **(photos 05 and 06)**. Add to the sauce and toss gently over medium heat, taking care not to break the Daikon Fettucine. Cook just until heated through, about 1 minute. Divide among individual plates, teasing the fettuccine into mounds. Serve immediately.

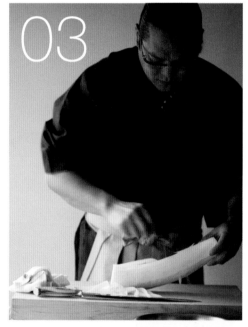
03

04

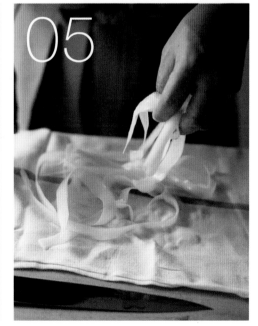
05

06

171

Eggplant Shigiyaki Morimoto-Style

Makes 4 servings

½ pound (225 g) ground chicken

2 tablespoons vegetable oil, plus more for deep-frying

2 cups Red Miso Sauce (page 259)

2 tablespoons sake

2 tablespoons soy sauce

3 or 4 small Italian eggplants, (1¼ pounds/575 g)

4 ounces (100 g) fresh mozzarella, thinly sliced

1 tablespoon minced chives

Here's my take on eggplant Parmesan—minus the Parmesan. Red Miso Sauce with ground chicken takes the place of tomato meat sauce, and strips of fried eggplant replace the traditional Italian slices. Slices of milky mozzarella blanket the top.

1. Preheat the oven to 375°F (190°C). In a medium skillet, cook the ground chicken in 2 tablespoons of oil over medium heat, stirring to break up the meat, until the chicken turns white and is cooked through, about 2 to 3 minutes.

2. Add the Red Miso Sauce, sake, and soy sauce to the pan and cook for 2 minutes. Remove from heat.

3. Peel the eggplants and cut into slices ½-inch (1 cm) thick. Pat dry with paper towels. In a deep-fryer or heavy saucepan, heat 2 inches (5 cm) of oil to 340°F (175°C).

4. Add the eggplant to the hot oil in 2 to 3 batches without crowding and fry until just tender and lightly browned, about 2 minutes. With a skimmer or slotted spoon, transfer the cooked eggplant to a strainer. Pour 1 cup of boiling water over the fried eggplant to remove excess oil. Pat dry.

5. Add the eggplant to the miso sauce and toss to coat completely. Spread out the eggplant in a 1-quart (1 liter) gratin or shallow casserole, or divide among 4 individual ramekins. Top with the mozzarella. (The recipe can be prepared to this point up to a day in advance.)

6. Bake for 5 to 7 minutes, or until the cheese is melted and lightly browned. Garnish with a sprinkling of chives.

Gammo Tofu Steak

Makes 4 servings

package (16 ounces/450 g)
firm tofu, drained and cut into
large dice

ounces (225 g) shrimp,
shelled, deveined, rinsed,
and coarsely chopped

cup peeled, grated
Japanese mountain potato*

egg white

teaspoon salt

teaspoon freshly ground
pepper

cup finely diced, peeled
fresh lotus root

vegetable oil

cup all-purpose flour

tablespoons Garlic-Soy Jus
(page 152)

tablespoon grated daikon,
for garnish

What may sound like humble ingredients belie the irresistible taste of this simple dish. The traditional way to supply texture to the creamy tofu cake is through the addition of boiled chicken cartilage. This recipe uses crisp chunks of lotus root to add crunch to the savory shrimp-flavored tofu.

Note: The plate at left shows the entire recipe made into one loaf. At home, it's much easier to cook the Gammo Tofu Steak formed into four patties.

1. Put the tofu, shrimp, mountain potato, egg white, salt, and pepper into a food processor. Purée until very smooth.

2. Turn the mixture into a bowl. Stir in the diced lotus root. Dip your hands in vegetable oil to prevent sticking and form the tofu purée into 4 oval patties 1 inch (2½ cm) thick. Refrigerate for at least 30 minutes or up to 1 hour.

3. Dust each patty lightly with flour. Add enough vegetable oil to a large sauté pan or skillet to coat it with a heavy film. Heat over medium heat until the oil is hot but not smoking.

4. Add the patties to the pan carefully and fry over medium heat until golden brown on the bottom, 2 minutes. Turn the patties over and cook until they are lightly browned on the second side, about 2 minutes. Continue to cook, turning the patties gently to prevent scorching, until they are golden brown all over and cooked through, 2 minutes longer.

5. Serve hot, drizzled with the Garlic-Soy Jus and garnished with grated daikon.

*Note: The "rough side" of a Japanese grater yields very fine, creamy pieces of mountain potato. A Japanese grater resembles a small dustpan covered with perforations. Proper grating technique is a circular motion.

When it is grated, mountain potato gives off a thick, sticky, very starchy liquid that can cause a skin rash on people who are allergic to it. To avoid any possible irritation when working with the vegetable, use thin, inexpensive surgical gloves, available at any pharmacy.

Foie Gras Chawanmushi

Makes 4 servings

A *chawan* is the traditional cup or small bowl used in the Japanese tea ceremony. Baking this simple, elegant custard in a gracefully shaped cup enhances the pleasure of your guests. The custard is served right from the baking cup, with a little clear sauce spooned on top. Since the custard is so rich, portions are small.

2 cups Shanton Broth (page 256)

8 ounces (225 g) fresh foie gras, at room temperature

Salt and freshly ground white pepper

4 large eggs

1 cup Dashi (page 256)

2 tablespoons mirin

2 tablespoons light-colored soy sauce

1 tablespoon cornstarch, dissolved in 1 tablespoon water

1 teaspoon grated fresh wasabi

1 teaspoon finely minced chives

1. Preheat the oven to 350°F (180°C).

2. Place the Shanton Broth and foie gras in a blender or food processor. Add a large pinch of salt and white pepper. Blend for about 20 seconds, until smooth. Add the eggs one at a time and pulse briefly after each addition. The eggs should be thoroughly combined without creating a great dea of foam; do not overprocess.

3. Strain the foie-gras custard through a fine mesh sieve into a medium bowl. Ladle the custard into four 6-ounce (175 g) heatproof custard cups or ramekins. Place them in a baking pan and add enough hot water to the pan to reach halfway up the cups. Cover the baking pan tightly with aluminum foil.

4. Bake the custards for 12 to 15 minutes, until they are set in the center.

5. While the custards are baking, make the sauce: Combin the Dashi, mirin, and soy sauce in a small saucepan. Bring to a simmer. Whisk in the dissolved cornstarch and bring to a boil, whisking until thickened. Remove from the heat.

6. Carefully remove each custard cup from the water bath and dry the bottom. Place each on a serving plate. Spoon 1 to 2 tablespoons of sauce over each custard and sprinkle with grated wasabi and minced chives. Serve immediately.

Vegetables, Tofu, and Eggs

Tempura Vegetables with XO Dipping Sauce

Makes 4 servings

Freshly fried vegetables in a light tempura batter are a favorite in Japan. I try to mix it up with a few surprises, but you can substitute almost any mushroom or firm vegetable you have on hand. Just try for a mix of colors and textures.

4 large royal trumpet mushrooms, or large shiitake or oyster mushrooms

8 asparagus spears

4 celery hearts

1 small butternut squash, peeled

Two 4- to 5-inch (10 to 12 cm) pieces of burdock root

2 quarts vegetable oil

2 cups all-purpose flour

4 cups Tempura Batter (page 260)

XO Dipping Sauce

....

XO DIPPING SAUCE

Makes about 2 cups

4 tablespoons vegetable oil

2 bunches of Tokyo scallions, white parts only, finely chopped

1 cup *XO Jan* (Chinese hot chile sauce, available in Asian specialty stores)

4 tablespoons sake

4 tablespoons oyster sauce

4 tablespoons soy sauce

4 teaspoons sugar

1. Cut the mushrooms in half so you have 4 pieces. Trim the asparagus to about 5 or 6 inches (12 to 15 cm). Trim the celery hearts and cut each stalk in half. Cut the squash into sticks about 4-inches (10 cm) long and ½-inch (1 cm) thick. Peel the burdock root and cut lengthwise into 4 long slices.

2. Heat the oil in a deep-fryer or large, heavy saucepan and bring to 350°F (180°C), or smoking.

3. In batches without crowding, dredge the vegetables in the flour, shake off excess, then dip in the Tempura Batter to coat. Add to the hot oil and fry until crisp, about 1 minute (except for the burdock, which takes 2 minutes). As the pieces are cooked, drain on paper towels, then arrange on a heatproof platter. Keep warm in a low oven while you fry the remaining batches.

4. Serve hot, with small bowls of XO Dipping Sauce.

XO Dipping Sauce

1. In a medium skillet, heat the oil over medium heat. Add the scallions and XO sauce and cook until the scallions soften, 1 to 2 minutes. Remove from the heat and scrape into a small bowl.

2. Stir in the sake, oyster sauce, soy sauce, and sugar.

Tofu

I realize that the prospect of tofu doesn't exactly set all of my customers' pulses racing. Certainly not like the prospect of my Toro Tartare crowned with Osetra caviar or the slab of pork belly that I braise for ten hours. Perhaps it never will. But freshly made tofu is one of the great pleasures of the table. In Japan, there are shops and even restaurants that specialize in making and serving fresh tofu. It tastes mild, faintly sweet, but what I really can't get enough of is its *shita-zawari*, the way it feels in your mouth—slick, creamy, fragile. The Japanese admire certain foods as much for their texture as for their taste: Tofu is one of those foods. I think fresh tofu has a mild, distinctly pleasant, almost sweet taste.

Long ago, nearly every town in Japan had a shop that sold freshly made tofu, which was ladled into bowls the shoppers brought with them. The best I have ever eaten is the tofu I bought as a child from a shop near my home; it was made fresh each morning. This is the tofu I wanted to recreate for my customers, to show them that the leaden pasty blocks sold in supermarkets do not represent all tofu. So before I opened my first restaurant, I asked a tofu maker to develop a method that would allow me to make it right at the table. It may not taste exactly the same as the tofu I loved as a child, but it is far superior to the commercial bricks.

By incorporating this bit of theater in my Tableside Tofu (see photos 01–03 on page 180), I can capture my customer's minds, if only for a few minutes, so they're forced to reconsider their notion of the product. Instead of a cold, firm slab, at my restaurants you get a large earthenware bowl filled with pale white soy milk heated to 160°F (70°C), which gives off a sweet, earthy aroma. Your waiter pours in *nigari*, a natural coagulant derived from seawater, gently stirring it, then covering the bowl. He returns in ten minutes to reveal that, magically, the liquid has become a delicate, wobbly custard.

Tofu this good needs little embellishment, so I usually serve it with fresh wasabi and *dashi*-spiked soy sauce, and lobster and mushroom *ankake*, stock thickened with a bit of starch. During white-truffle season, however, I can't help myself: I serve the fresh tofu plain, with a light sprinkling of sea salt. Then I grate paper-thin slices of the fragrant tuber over the tofu.

Tofu originated in China, where so many different foods are made from the soybean that it acquired the affectionate nickname, "the cow of China."

Soybean curd was probably introduced to Japan in the 8th century, though it did not receive its modern Japanese name, "tofu," until the 12th century. Many people credit its migration to Buddhist monks, whose vegetarian cuisine, or *shojin ryori*, was dependent on soy as a protein substitute for meat. Only after several centuries in Japan did the technique for making it pass down from this rarefied class to ordinary citizens. Far from being treated as simply

Tofu

a substitute for meat, tofu was embraced by carnivores and vegetarians alike for its subtle sweetness and satiny texture.

You're probably familiar with edamame, the green pods that many Japanese restaurants give you at the beginning of a meal. The smooth, pale green beans inside these pods are fresh, young soybeans; tofu is made from mature soybeans that have been dried, known as *daizu*. To make these into tofu, they are soaked overnight in water, ground, and boiled in more water. The resulting thick concoction is drained, so it separates into soy milk (*tonyu*) and soy lees (*okara*).

In a process similar to cheese-making, a coagulant is added to the milk to form curds. Traditionally, this is *nigari* as mentioned above, but now most tofu is made using chemical approximations. Usually packed in water, this soft, wobbly

tofu, called *kinu dofu*, or "silken tofu," is ready to be eaten. In Japan, cooks top *kinu dofu* with sliced scallions, finely grated ginger, and soy sauce, or float pieces of silken tofu in miso soup. Silken tofu also makes a good nondairy medium in desserts and dressings. Firmer tofu, which comes in blocks, has had most of the water pressed out of it and is used in a wide variety of ways: fired, baked, simmered, and grilled.

The Japanese are not the only lovers of tofu. The Koreans and Chinese, just to name two, consume tofu voraciously. I love Korean tofu stews, like *soon dubu chigae*, for which tofu provides a creamy, cooling counterpoint to fiery kimchi. And I love the Chinese dish *ma po tofu*, simmered tofu laced with ground pork and chile-bean paste. In fact, I'm so mad about it that I've included my recipe for it on page 182.

Chef Morimoto prepares his
Tableside Tofu, shown on
page 179.

Tofu and Spicy Pork Sauce

with Crispy Fried Rice

Makes 4 servings

1 large, or 2 medium, dried shiitake mushroom(s)

1 tablespoon vegetable oil

1 tablespoon finely chopped garlic

1 tablespoon finely chopped peeled fresh ginger

1 scallion, white and green separated, finely chopped

1 tablespoon finely chopped bamboo shoot

1 tablespoon finely chopped celery

12 ounces (350 g) ground pork

1 cup Shanton Broth or Chicken Stock (page 256)

1 tablespoon red miso

1 tablespoon Chinese hot chile sauce (tobanjan)

1 tablespoon sugar

1 tablespoon soy sauce

2 teaspoons cornstarch, dissolved in 1 tablespoon water

1 pound (450 g) firm tofu, diced

Crispy Rice

Sesame oil, for garnish

Scallion, sliced, for garnish

....

CRISPY RICE

Makes about 1 cup

2 cups steamed rice

Vegetable oil, for deep-frying

Everyone loves this recipe, which they know from Chinese restaurants as *Ma Po Tofu*. It's a versatile dish, which here is served over crispy rice. You could also serve it over noodles. For a change, I sometimes like to fry cooked rice until it's crispy and sprinkle it on top, instead.

1. Soak the shiitake mushroom in hot water to cover until soft, about 20 minutes. Drain and squeeze to remove as much liquid as possible. Remove the stem and finely chop the mushroom cap.

2. In a large skillet, heat the oil over medium heat. Add the garlic, ginger, white part of the scallion, bamboo shoot, celery, and chopped shiitake mushroom. Cook, stirring often, until the garlic is tender, 2 to 3 minutes.

3. Add the pork, raise the heat to medium-high, and sauté, breaking up any lumps of meat with the side of a spoon, until it is cooked through with no trace of pink, about 7 minutes. Add the Shanton Broth, red miso, *tobanjan*, sugar, and soy sauce and bring to a boil. Stir in the dissolved cornstarch and cook, stirring, until thickened, about 30 seconds. (The pork sauce can be made up to 1 day ahead, cooled, covered, and refrigerated. Reheat gently in a skillet.)

4. Shortly before serving, add the tofu to the pork sauce, and stir gently to mix. Cook until it is heated through, about 3 minutes. Serve in bowls with the Crispy Rice. Top with a drizzle of sesame oil and a little sliced scallion.

Crispy Rice

1. Preheat the oven to 200°F (90°C). Line a baking sheet with parchment or waxed paper. Spread out the rice on the sheet. Bake for 1 hour, stirring occasionally. Turn off the heat and let the rice continue to dry in the oven for at least 8 hours or overnight. Set the dried rice aside at room temperature for up to 12 hours until ready to fry the rice.

2. To fry the rice, heat about 2 inches (5 cm) of oil in a large saucepan. In batches, carefully add a handful of rice to the oil and fry until golden, about 2 minutes. Using a fine wire mesh skimmer or a heatproof (no plastic) wire sieve, scoop out the rice and drain on paper towels.

Sushi Omelet

Makes 6 to 8 servings

½ cup **Dashi** (page 256)

½ cup **sugar**

1½ tablespoons **sake**

1½ tablespoons **mirin**

12 **eggs**

Vegetable oil

While this rolled omelet looks tricky, it's something every Japanese home cook knows how to make. All you need is the special pan (see Sources, page 265) and a little practice. Of course, here at the restaurant, we supersize it to make enough for our sushi service. This sushi omelet adds an extra color to a sushi platter. The taste of the sushi omelet always indicates how good a sushi restaurant is.

1. In a small saucepan, combine the Dashi, sugar, sake, and mirin. Bring to a boil, stirring to dissolve the sugar. Boil for 1 minute longer to make sure all the alcohol is evaporated. Remove from the heat and let cool for 5 to 10 minutes.

2. In a large bowl, whisk the eggs to beat lightly. Gradually beat in the Dashi mixture, whisking until very well blended. Strain through a fine sieve into another bowl or a large glass measuring cup; the cup will be easier for home cooks, because you can pour and measure at the same time.

3. Lightly oil a 10½ x 10½ inch (25 x 25 cm) Japanese omelet pan and place over medium-high heat. When the pan is very hot, ladle or pour in about ⅛ of the egg mixture, quickly tilt the pan so the eggs coat the bottom in a thin layer. Cook until the eggs are beginning to set but are still runny on top **(photo 01)**, 20 seconds.

4. Tilt the pan toward you and use chopsticks or a spatula to help the eggs begin to roll. Fold the omelet in thirds like a letter, moving the cooked omelet in the top of the pan. Lightly oil the bottom of the pan. Ladle or pour in another ⅛ of the eggs

(photo 02) and quickly tilt to cover the bottom, lifting the cooking omelet with chopsticks or a spatula so some of the uncooked egg can run under **(photo 03)**. Tilt the pan in the opposite direction and roll the omelet back on itself **(photo 04)**. At home, you'll want to use chopsticks or a spatula and a tilted skillet to accomplish this. Professionals flip the omelet right in the pan **(photo 05)**. Repeat six more times with the remaining egg mixture, oiling the pan only when necessary to prevent sticking.

5. When all the egg has been cooked, unmold the omelet onto a platter. At the restaurant, we make such a large omelet that we use a special board to hold it **(photo 06)**. Let the omelet cool before slicing. The sweet egg omelet is traditionally served at room temperature.

06

Caramelized Sweet Potato

Makes 4 to 6 servings

2 pounds (900 g) Japanese sweet potatoes, or red-skinned yams

Vegetable oil, for frying

½ cup sugar

2 tablespoons minced fresh chervil, or parsley, for garnish

1 tablespoon black sesame seeds, for garnish

We serve these instead of French fries in the restaurant, and most people can't get enough of them. We dip each candied potato stick briefly in ice water to make the caramel coating crisp and brittle.

1. Peel the sweet potatoes, leaving some strips of skin intact for color and a crispy texture. Cut the potatoes into sticks 3- to 4-inches (7 to 10 cm) long and ½-inch (1 cm) thick. Rinse them quickly in cold water to remove excess surface starch, drain and pat dry thoroughly on paper towels.

2. In a deep-fryer or large heavy saucepan, heat at least 1½ inches (4 cm) of oil to 340°F (170°C). In several batches without crowding, carefully add the sweet potato sticks to the hot oil. Stir gently with a slotted spoon or chopsticks to ensure the potatoes cook evenly. Fry them until crisp and lightly colored, about 4 minutes, or when a skewer pierces smoothly inside. Drain on paper towels and set aside in a shallow bowl.

3. Combine the sugar and 2 tablespoons of water into a small nonstick skillet. Set over medium-high heat and bring to a boil, stirring to dissolve the sugar. Continue to cook without stirring, carefully swirling the liquid to make sure it cooks evenly, until the syrup turns a light caramel color, about 4 to 6 minutes.

4. Remove the pan from the heat and carefully pour the caramel over the potatoes. Toss with a wooden spoon or chopsticks to coat evenly. Transfer the potatoes to a lightly oiled plate. Garnish with chopped chervil leaves and black sesame seeds. Serve immediately.

Frozen Lettuce

Makes 4 servings

1 head of iceberg lettuce

3 garlic cloves

¼ cup vegetable oil

1 egg yolk

½ cup mayonnaise

2 tablespoons rice vinegar

1 tablespoon fresh lemon juice

1 tablespoon Worcestershire sauce

1 tablespoon white miso

1 tablespoon grated onion

1 tablespoon grated Parmesan

1 tablespoon anchovy paste

½ teaspoon yellow mustard

Zest of 1 lemon

Salt and freshly ground black pepper

1 tablespoon crumbled goat cheese

Annatto seeds, for garnish, optional

Small croutons, for garnish

I'd be willing to wager you've never had a salad like this one, and neither have your guests. It's sort of a whimsical play on Caesar salad that defies expectations. Whatever you think of it, this is guaranteed to be a conversation piece.

1. Quarter the lettuce. Wrap the pieces in plastic or seal in a covered container and freeze for 1 to 2 hours.

2. In a small saucepan of boiling water, cook the garlic cloves for 5 minutes; drain. Mince the garlic.

3. In a small bowl, whisk the oil into the egg yolk. Whisk in the garlic, mayonnaise, vinegar, lemon juice, Worcestershire sauce, miso, grated onion, Parmesan, anchovy paste, mustard, and lemon zest. Season the dressing with salt and pepper to taste. Fold in the crumbled goat cheese.

4. Place the frozen lettuce on four chilled plates. Spoon the dressing over the lettuce and garnish with a sprinkling of annatto seeds and croutons. Serve immediately.

Curried Mushroom Salad

Makes 4 servings

I choose mushrooms according to the season. Of course, when wonderful wild mushrooms like *matsutake* are in season, that's when you're most likely to find me making this dish. It can be served Japanese style on its own as a tasty appetizer or small dish, or used in a more Western-style menu as an interesting side dish to dress up a simple main course, like roast chicken or leg of lamb. You can eat the salad with a fork and knife, or the endive can be used as a spoon.

3 tablespoons unsalted butter

1 shallot, minced

1 garlic clove, minced

¾ pound (350 g) mixed fresh mushrooms (*matsutake*, shiitake, oyster, enoki, or any other), diced

1 cup steamed white rice

2 tablespoons dry white wine

2 tablespoons Madras curry powder

Salt and freshly ground black pepper

1 Belgian endive, separated into leaves

2 tablespoons minced chives, for garnish

1. In a large sauté pan or skillet, melt the butter over medium-high heat. Add the shallot, garlic, and mushrooms and sauté until the mushrooms begin to soften, 2 to 3 minutes

2. Stir in the steamed rice and continue cooking for 2 minutes over medium heat. Add the white wine, then stir in the curry powder. Toss well. Season with salt and pepper to taste.

3. Arrange the endive leaves on 4 plates. Spoon the mushroom salad onto the leaves. Garnish with the chives.

Recipes to Contemplate

Morimoto Sashimi and Toro Tartare

I put my signature on this geometric sashimi (left) by molding it inside a rectangular box and serving it with an array of sauces of various colors and flavors. That way people get to play a little, and mix and match according to their own taste preferences. Sauces include: barbecued eel sauce, arugula sauce, roasted yellow pepper sauce, Yuzu Vinaigrette (see page 68), and *tamari* soy sauce.

Toro Tartare (right) is one of the ultraluxurious sashimi dishes I like to assemble at my restaurants. It looks striking and tastes heavenly. Plus it's a lot of fun to eat. The diner uses the wooden paddles to mix and match the Toro Tartare with any of the garnishes (from left: nori, sour cream, guacamole, *benitade*, chives, wasabi, and rice cracker.) In addition, there is a small plate of dashi-soy sauce. This is a dish you could actually replicate at home.

Blowfish Skin Caprese

Makes 4 servings

Blowfish *(fugu)* is not only hard to come by and very expensive, but you cannot prepare it without a license so I've substituted monkfish here. *Fugu* is a Japanese fish, and therefore specific to Japanese cusine, but I intentionally incorporate Italian ingredients to make this dish unusual. Fresh mozzarella and sweet tomatoes, as well as extra virgin olive oil and basil, lend the "Caprese" to this dish.

Skin of 1 medium monkfish

4 bocconcini (small balls of fresh mozzarella), quartered

1 Japanese fruit tomato or medium heirloom tomato, diced

2 tablespoons extra virgin olive oil

1 tablespoon light-colored soy sauce

1 tablespoon *kabosu* or fresh lime juice

Sea salt and cracked black peppercorns

1 tablespoon micro basil or slivered fresh basil

1. Peel the skin off the monkfish: To do so, first remove the bone. Place the deboned fillet skin side down on a cutting board and slip a knife between the fish and the skin. Then slide the knife down the skin while pulling the skin back with your other hand; the skin should come off in one piece.

2. In a medium saucepan of boiling salted water, blanch the monkfish skin until tender, 1 to 2 minutes. Drain immediately and rinse under cold running water until cool. Cut the fish skin into very thin strips 1-inch (2½ cm) long.

3. In a small bowl, toss the strips of fish skin with the mozzarella, tomato, olive oil, soy sauce, and *kabosu* juice. Season with salt and pepper to taste.

4. Divide the salad among 4 small bowls or plates. Top each with a sprinkling of basil.

Sweetfish and Rice

Makes 4 servings

The sweetfish *(ayu)* referred to in the title, is a freshwater fish highly prized for its delicate, almost fruity flavor. Because it is so dear, it is usually combined with a mild-flavored rice, as it is here, so every diner gets a nice portion of rice and a little fish. You can make this same preparation with another light fish, but the flavor will not be quite the same.

3 cups short-grain white rice

3 cups Dashi (page 256)

4 whole sweetfish *(ayu)*, gutted and cleaned

Coarse salt

1 teaspoon light-colored soy sauce

2 tablespoons sake

4 sprigs of *kinome*

1 teaspoon grated *yuzu*, or lemon zest

1. Rinse the rice well by swishing it in a bowl of cold water and draining it in a sieve. Repeat until the water is clear. Let the rice stand for 30 to 60 minutes—shorter in summer, longer in the winter because then the rice is harder.

2. Put the soaked rice into a heavy saucepan wide enough to accommodate the fish and add the Dashi.

3. Meanwhile, prepare the fish: *Ayu*, or sweetfish, has a protective layer of slime covering its skin. You must remove this by rubbing the fish with coarse salt in a bowl of cold water or in a colander under cold running water. When the skin no longer feels slippery, pat the fish dry with paper towels. Salt lightly all over, making sure to cover the fins and tail and getting some salt in the gills.

4. Preheat the broiler. Grill the whole fish about 4 inches from the heat, turning once, for about 3½ minutes per side to brown the skin. Remove the fish to a plate.

5. Season the rice with the soy sauce, sake, and salt to taste. Set the broiled fish on top of the rice, cover the pan tightly with a lid, and bring to a boil over high heat. When you see steam escaping from the lid, reduce the heat to medium and cook for 10 to 12 minutes.

6. Remove from the heat and let stand, covered, for 10 minutes. To serve, remove the fish and separate the fillets. Divide the rice among 4 bowls. Place pieces of the fish on top and garnish with the *kinome* and grated *yuzu* zest.

Baby White Shrimp and Sea Urchin

Makes 4 servings

Full of sea flavor, this elegant sashimi dish contrasts the brisk briny flavor of sea urchin *(uni)* with the mildness of baby white shrimp. Both ingredients are "sweet" and both are soft in different ways, which makes it a sensuous dish that calls for attention.

½ cup baby white shrimp *(shiraebi)*

½ cup sea urchin *(uni)*

About 12 Japanese baby chives *(menegi),* cut into 1-inch (2½ cm) lengths

2 teaspoons grated fresh wasabi

1. With a large sharp knife, chop the shrimp to make a coarse paste. A food processor will make the texture of the shrimp too smooth.

2. Arrange ¼ of the *uni* to fill half of 4 small dishes. Spoon the shrimp purée next to the *uni* to fill the other half of each dish.

3. Garnish each dish with a small bundle of *menegi* and ½ teaspoon grated fresh wasabi. Serve immediately.

Blowfish and Other Ingredients from Japan

As part of my quest for perfection in food, I go through great lengths to find the best ingredients I can, often buying directly from Japan. Yet I don't source from my home country simply for effect; I do it because I think *matsutake* mushrooms grown there taste better than those grown in the United States. The same goes for wasabi. There are other ingredients you just can't get from anywhere else, like *fugu* (blowfish), *ayu* (sweetfish), and *kinome*, which you'll find fresh at only a handful of restaurants in the United States.

FUGU

Since I love to think of dining as theater, *fugu* seems like a fish that was made for me. The organs and blood of fugu, or blowfish, contains tetrodotoxin, a poison more powerful than cyanide. One bite of sloppily prepared *fugu*, and you'll have less than an hour to regret it. What else says high drama like the prospect of danger and the adrenaline rush it provides?

But, of course, *fugu* is completely safe. If it wasn't, I wouldn't even consider offering it in my restaurants. Chefs who are allowed to gut, clean, and fillet *fugu* must go through rigorous training and obtain a special license. They even go so far as to discard the poison parts in a locked box so they cannot be consumed by accident. Indeed, almost all of the deaths that occur as a result of eating *fugu* happen outside of restaurants.

In Japan, there are over a thousand restaurants with chefs that have the certification required to serve *fugu*. To celebrate the season, which begins in November and ends in March, many of them create wildly expensive meals focused on the fish, where some part of it shows up in every course. It's served every which way: raw, deep-fried, cooked briefly in simmering broth. There's even *hire-zake*—a drink of charred, dried *fugu* fin steeped in hot sake, which I serve during *fugu* season. All of it is delicious, though sometimes I wonder whether mild-tasting *fugu* would be as sought after if it didn't have its menacing aura or its prohibitive price.

Fugu could not always be imported into the United States. Years ago, a Japanese chef in New York worked out a deal with the FDA that allowed him to import *fugu* that had already been prepared by licensed chefs. Now, the only way to get it is to join a special organization, of which there are only few members in the United States.

Because of its slightly tough texture, fugu needs to be cut into extremely thin, translucent slices before being served as sashimi, a style of cutting called *usuzukuri*. To accomplish this, I use a particularly thin knife made especially for *fugu*. Then I arrange the delicate pieces on a plate, like the petals of a flower. Instead of a simple Ponzu Sauce (see page 260), I purée the tart condiment with rich monkfish liver. My customers dig in as if they're not afraid, but I think that their first bite brings with it an exhilarating tickle of fear that piques the appetite.

AYU

Another beloved seasonal fish, *ayu*, also called "sweetfish," is caught in rivers throughout Japan starting in early summer. Though some people covet the female fish late in the season, when she's heavy with roe, I prefer the unadulterated young fish. You can taste the impact of the *ayu*'s diet on its flesh. *Ayu* live for only one year, and during its short life, the fish feasts on mosslike plants that cling to rocks in the river, which impart a beguiling flavor reminiscent of cucumber or melon.

Fishermen employ two unusual methods for catching *ayu*. For the first, they tie the throats of cormorants so they can't swallow, and send these birds out to fish for *ayu*. Then the fish are collected from the birds' beaks. This method, however, is rarely, if ever, used nowadays for anything but a show for tourists. The second and more common method is called *tomo-zuri*, and it exploits the extremely territorial nature of *ayu*. Fishermen bait their hooks with live *ayu* and cast them into the river, sending the fish there into a furor. When the free *ayu* attack to defend their territory, the crafty fishermen get a bite.

Ideally, we would ship our morning haul by plane to Tokyo to be sold at the giant Tsukiji market, where it would bring the highest price. If we missed the plane, sometimes we would have to send the *matsutake* to Osaka, where it sold for much less. Overcome by the pressure of shipping on time and figuring out where to sell and for how much, the stress of marketing these pricey mushrooms often gave my boss nosebleeds.

I hope this never affected his ability to smell *matsutake* because, above their elegant, earthy taste and meaty texture, they are mainly prized for their irresistible woodsy aroma. In Japan, they say, "Taste *shimeji* [another type of mushroom], smell *matsutake.*" One of the best ways to experience *matsutake* is in clear broth served in a lidded bowl or teapot that's uncovered by the diner just before eating. This way, you get the full impact of its aroma.

JAPANESE HERBS

Diners count on seeing mint and kaffir lime leaves scattered in their Thai salads or cilantro on their tacos, but not many expect to find a lot of herbs at a Japanese-inspired restaurant. Yet I love to use herbs in my cooking. That tangle of greens on my octopus carpaccio? It's *mitsuba*, an herb whose taste hints at parsley and celery, wilted from a splash of scalding oil. That dainty, fernlike sprig perched on top of steamed fresh bamboo shoots or steeped in a sauce of soy and mirin that dresses grilled quail? It's *kinome*, the young leaves of the *sansho* plant (whose seeds are ground to use as pepper), and it lends a pleasantly astringent sensation, like a merging of lemon zest and mint.

Of course, I also use the more common *shiso*, the large, jagged-edged green leaf reminiscent of spearmint, but unlike most chefs, I use it in its infant form, when it's just a purplish bud *(shisonomi)*. I sprinkle these over Lamb Carpaccio (see page 162) and the *fugu* dish just mentioned, to provide a delicious peppery bite.

At my restaurants, we rub the fish with salt and grill it whole, a popular technique called *shioyaki*. In my book, however, I've provided a less traditional way to enjoy it: candied ayu livers, braised in a soy- and sake-based sauce, and dipped in dark chocolate.

MATSUTAKE

While I was an apprentice at Ichiban Zushi, a small restaurant in Hiroshima where I got my grounding in Japanese cooking, my boss operated a side business selling *matsutake*, a luxurious mushroom that I, along with every other Japanese person I know, adore. Actually, this project kept him—and by association, me—so busy that sometimes I wondered whether the side business was the mushroom-selling or the sushi bar.

In the morning, he would send me hours away to the forests in Hiroshima to buy these fat-stemmed mushrooms, which grow wild beneath pine trees in the fall (*matsu* means "pine," *take* means "mushroom"). Like truffles, *matsutake* tend to grow in the same place year after year, and foragers guard these spots vigilantly. Also, like truffles, they command high prices, sometimes over a hundred dollars per mushroom. Because of its popularity, the *matsutake* grown in Japan can't feed all lovers of this fabulous mushroom, so they are also imported from Korea and the U.S. Pacific Northwest.

Kinki with Perigeux Sauce

Makes 2 to 4 servings

A traditional method of preserving fish is to dry it in the sun for a day, which I do for this recipe. Although I use *kinki*, a special fish imported from Japan, I incorporate the traditionally French Perigeux Sauce for an interesting twist. Note that *kombu* is added to the water the fish is soaked in, to subtly release its natural MSG, which heightens the flavor of the fish.

2 whole *kinki*, about 1 pound (450 g) each

2 tablespoons coarse salt

1 piece of *kombu*, about 4-inches (10 cm) square

½ cup Perigeux Sauce

Sudachi wedges, for garnish

....

PERIGEUX SAUCE

Makes about ½ cup

1 shallot, minced

2 tablespoons olive oil

2 white button mushrooms, sliced

¼ teaspoon black peppercorns

1 sprig of fresh thyme

1 tablespoon balsamic vinegar

1 cup Madeira

1 cup port

1 cup Veal Stock (page 257) or canned beef broth

1 teaspoon cornstarch mixed with 2 teaspoons water, optional

1 tablespoon unsalted butter

1 tablespoon minced black truffle, fresh or preserved

Salt and freshly ground black pepper

1. Make sure the fish are well cleaned. In a large bowl, dissolve the salt in 4 cups cold water. Add the *kombu* and the whole fish and let soak for 1 hour.

2. Remove the fish from the water and dry throughly with paper towels. Transfer to a plate and let it dry in the sun for a day.

3. Preheat the broiler. Grill the fish 4 inches (10 cm) from the heat for 4 to 5 minutes on each side, until the skin is crisp and the flesh is just opaque.

4. Drizzle about 2 tablespoons of the rich Perigeux Sauce over and around each fish. Garnish with *sudachi* wedges. Serve immediately.

Perigeux Sauce

1. In a heavy, medium saucepan cook the shallot in the olive oil over medium heat until softened, about 2 minutes. Add the sliced mushrooms, peppercorns, and thyme.

2. Pour in the balsamic vinegar, Madeira, and port and boil until the liquid is thick and bubbling. Add the Veal Stock and boil until reduced by half, or until the sauce is thick enough to coat a spoon. If the sauce is not thick enough, stir in the dissolved cornstarch and return to a boil, whisking until thickened, about 1 minute. Strain through a fine sieve, pressing on the solids to extract as much liquid as possible.

3. Shortly before serving, reheat the sauce over medium heat until it is barely simmering. Remove from the heat and whisk in the butter 1 tablespoon at a time, until just melted. Stir in the truffle. Season with salt and pepper to taste.

Caviar Tempura

Makes 4 servings

Tempura is more of a conceit here, but the term does indicate how these delicate pouches, filled with luscious caviar, are briefly fried. While the special sheets of *obrato*, a clear gel made of soy lecithin, look like plastic wrap, the ingredient is completely edible. In fact, the delicate wrapping melts in your mouth. Here, the luxurious pouches are served on top of Lemon Cream and garnished with chives.

4 sheets of Japanese soy lecithin *(obrato)*

1 tablespoon extra virgin olive oil

4 teaspoons Osetra caviar or American sturgeon row

½ cup tempura batter

Vegetable oil, for deep frying

4 tablespoons Lemon Cream (page 94)

Fresh chives, chopped, for garnish

1. Brush outer rim of the *obrato* sheets with olive oil. Place 1 teaspoon of the caviar in the center of each sheet. Pull up the sides, creating a pouch to enclose the caviar. Twist the ends of the pouch to seal.

2. In a deep-fryer or large deep saucepan, heat at least 2 inches (5 cm) of oil to 350°F (180°C). Lightly cover the caviar with the tempura batter. Fry the caviar pouches until crispy, about 30 to 45 seconds. Remove, drain briefly on a clean towel or paper napkins, and serve immediately, with a spoonful of Lemon Cream. Garnish with fresh chives.

Toro Prosciutto

Makes 4 servings

Here *otoro*, the fattiest, most desirable part of the tuna belly is first cured like salmon, then cold-smoked over wood chips. Cold-smoking involves a lower temperature and a longer time than ordinary smoking. The results are moister, saltier, and a bit smokier; but because it is trickier to control, cold-smoking is not something most people can do at home.

4 ounces (100 g) tuna belly **(otoro)**

¼ cup kosher salt

1 tablespoon sugar

¼ cup wood chips

½ pound (225 g) *udo*, or any vegetable, sliced into ribbons

1½ tablespoons best-quality extra virgin olive oil

½ ounce (12 g) fresh white truffle or 1½ teaspoons white truffle oil, optional

Sprigs of *kinome*, for garnish

1. Mix together the sugar and salt and cover the tuna with it. Allow the tuna to sit in the refrigerator for 24 hours.

2. Wash the tuna in cold water and pat dry with paper towels.

3. Cold-smoke the tuna for 5 to 10 minutes.

4. Place the tuna in the freezer to lightly freeze, making slicing easier, about 10 minutes. Thinly slice the fish into wide strips and serve slightly chilled over ribbons of *udo*. Drizzle lightly with olive oil and garnish with shavings of white truffle and *kinome*. Serve immediately.

Albalone Croquette

Makes 4 servings

Although this recipe calls for deep-fried croquettes, I deep-fry the whole shell at the restaurant, as pictured. Sprinkle with as much Parmesan as necessary for a sharp garnish.

1 good-size, live abalone in its shell

2 sea scallops

2 extra-large shrimp

1 tablespoon mayonnaise

½ teaspoon soy sauce

Juice of 1 *yuzu*, or 1½ tablespoons fresh lemon juice

½ teaspoon Dijon mustard

4 button mushrooms, diced

1 tablespoon unsalted butter

3 tablespoons dry white wine

Béchamel Sauce with Sautéed Onion

2 tablespoons boiled fresh or thawed frozen, shelled edamame

½ cup all-purpose flour

1 egg, beaten

1 cup Japanese bread crumbs (*panko*)

Vegetable oil, for deep frying

....

BECHAMEL SAUCE
WITH SAUTÉED ONION
Makes about ⅔ cup

¼ cup finely diced onion

1½ tablespoons butter

1 tablespoon all-purpose flour

¾ cup milk

½ teaspoon fresh lemon juice

Pinch of salt and cayenne pepper

1. Clean the abalone, separating the liver from the meat and reserving the bottom shell. Cut the abalone meat, scallops, and shrimp into ½-inch (12 mm) pieces. Set aside.

2. In a mini-food processor, combine the abalone liver, mayonnaise, soy sauce, *yuzu* juice, and mustard. Purée to make a smooth sauce. Set aside for dipping.

3. In a medium skillet, sauté the seafood pieces and mushrooms in the butter over high heat for 2 minutes. Pour in the wine. Cook, tossing, for 30 seconds. Transfer to a medium bowl. Add the Bechamel Sauce with Sautéed Onion and the edamame to the seafood and stir to mix evenly.

4. Stuff the seafood mixture into the abalone shell, mounding it as necessary. Coat the top with the flour, beaten egg, and *panko*. Fry in 350°F (180°C) oil until golden brown.

Bechamel Sauce with Sautéed Onion

1. In a small, heavy saucepan, cook the onion in the butter over medium heat until it is soft and translucent, 3 to 5 minutes.

2. Sprinkle in the flour and cook, stirring, for 1 to 2 minutes without allowing the flour to color.

3. Whisk in the milk and bring to a boil, whisking until the sauce is thickened and smooth. Reduce the heat to low and simmer, whisking occasionally, for 3 minutes. Season with the lemon juice, salt, and cayenne.

Wasabi

It should come as no surprise to anyone familiar with my food that I love wasabi. I've served it freshly grated with tofu and sashimi, fried its leaves into tempura, made pickles by soaking wasabi in sake, and whipped it into sorbet. I even named my restaurant in Mumbai after it. One reason I enjoy using this bewitching plant as much as I do is because each dish in which it is included brings the opportunity for my customers to have a taste epiphany. You see, most Americans have never had real wasabi, let alone the freshly grated stuff.

So I surprise many of my customers when I show them fresh wasabi, the bright green, knobby rhizome that they typically see only in paste form. They are surprised again when they taste it. In most Japanese restaurants, the pale green lump that comes with your sushi is not fresh wasabi. Some products sold as "wasabi powder" are actually a mixture of horseradish, mustard, and green food coloring that contain no wasabi at all. Restaurants are reluctant to use real wasabi and especially fresh wasabi, because the real stuff doesn't come cheap. But the added expense makes for a huge difference in taste. Powdered wasabi tastes harsh and bitter; its sting is mighty, but it has little flavor. The fresh grated root, on the other hand, is a different animal, with a milder bite and a heady sweetness.

Most people know wasabi from the sushi bar. Like other sushi chefs, when I make *nigiri sushi,* I add a dab of grated wasabi between the fish and rice—just enough so that you sense its presence. Too much would disrupt the delicate balance of flavor. It is hard for me to imagine sushi without the tingle and sweetness of wasabi, but some believe that chefs paired wasabi with sushi early on because it provided a more practical service: killing bacteria in the days before refrigeration. The same is often said about chile peppers.

While in the United States grated wasabi is most commonly served with sushi and sashimi, I occasionally use it to supply a small explosion of flavor in other dishes, such as my Mashed Potato Soup (see page 86) , Snapper and Rice Soup (see page 90), and Foie Gras Chawanmushi (see page 176).

Wasabi has been a part of the Japanese pantry for hundreds of years. The wild plant grows slowly, high in the mountains of Japan, where it's harvested from the bottom of cold, shallow streams. It takes over a year to reach its mature size. Though its bite resembles that of horseradish—anyone who has eaten too much of either knows the result: a stinging pain that races into your sinuses, then leaves as quickly as it came—the two plants are not related. It's also cultivated in Japan, and recently, as a result of its increasing popularity, a few American farms have begun to grow it as well.

There are several different wasabi graters on the market. The best ones, and the type I use, is made with sharkskin attached to a wood paddle, but any grater will do in a pinch. If you're using a metal grater, whose teeth are too sharp for properly grating wasabi, you can cover it with aluminum foil to blunt them. To grate the root, I peel off its knobby outer layer and gently but firmly press the tip against the rough sharkskin. Then I move the root in tiny circles until it becomes a fine paste. Only then does its pungent flavor truly show itself.

If you are able to find fresh wasabi where you live, buy it. Ideally, choose fresh, firm rhizomes dotted with small bumps, though even when slightly past its prime, fresh wasabi beats the pants off the powdered substitute. Wrap it in a wet paper towel and store it in the refrigerator. The next best thing after the freshly grated rhizome is wasabi paste made with real wasabi. Just don't expect its flavor to come close.

Beef Belly Tartare with Truffled Egg Yolks

Makes 4 servings

4 ounces (100 g) boneless Wagyu beef belly short rib (sashimi quality)

1 teaspoon minced shallot

1 teaspoon finely diced celery

1 teaspoon minced fresh chives

1 garlic clove, minced

Pinch of Japanese yellow mustard

Aged soy sauce, 3-year-old

Sea salt and freshly ground black pepper

4 slices of Truffled Egg Yolks

1 tablespoon balsamic vinegar, reduced

1 tablespoon Chive Oil (page 259)

1 tablespoon white truffle oil

···························

TRUFFLED EGG YOLKS
Makes 4 yolks

4 whole eggs, preferably organic

2 pounds (900 g) white miso (*saikyo*, available in Asian specialty stores)

20 to 24 thin slices of fresh black truffle (about 1 ounce /25 g)

1 teaspoon white truffle oil

Japan's best Wagyu beef belly is high-quality enough to eat as a tartare—its fat content is melted away by its body temperature. I add fewer seasonings in my version of steak tartare than you'd find in a traditional one, though my secret ingredient is a special soy sauce that is aged for three years. Since I always like to put my signature on a classic dish, in place of the raw egg yolk that is often mixed into steak tartare, I serve my Beef Belly Tartare sprinkled with shredded dry red pepper and accompanied by a Truffled Egg Yolk.

1. Trim any fat or sinew from the beef. Finely dice the meat.

2. In a small bowl, lightly mix the meat with the shallot, celery, chives, garlic, mustard, soy sauce, and salt and pepper to taste.

3. Gently shape in a log on a plate. Arrange the truffled egg slices on top. Sprinkle with the balsamic vinegar, Chive Oil, and truffle oil.

Truffled Egg Yolks

1. In a small saucepan, poach the eggs at 150°F (65°C) for 1 hour.

2. Immediately shell the eggs and carefully remove the yolks from the whites; reserve the whites for another use. Marinate the egg yolks in the white miso in the refrigerator for 3 days.

3. Remove the egg yolks from the miso and carefully wipe with a paper towel. Sandwich each egg yolk between 4 truffle slices, 2 on top and 2 on the bottom. Top with a drizzle of truffle oil and seal in a vacuum bag, if possible; or wrap snugly in plastic wrap and seal in a zip-lock plastic bag. Marinate in the refrigerator for at least 3 days, or until ready to use.

Chocolate-Coated Sweetfish Liver

Makes 4 servings

French chefs contrast the unctuousness of foie gras with a brown sauce laced with chocolate. I dip sweetfish *(ayu)* livers in bittersweet couverature— a dish I created in an "Iron Chef" battle when the secret ingredient was *ayu*.

½ cup sake

4 very fresh sweetfish *(ayu)* livers

½ cup brandy

8 ounces (225 g) bittersweet chocolate, preferably bittersweet couvertare, melted

1. In a small saucepan, heat the sake, then carefully flame with a long match to burn off the alcohol.

2. Add the fish livers and simmer over low heat for 2 minutes. Transfer the livers to a shallow bowl and let cool.

3. Pour in the brandy and let the livers soak for 1 hour.

4. Melt the chocolate in a small bowl set over a pan of hot water. Skewer each liver and dip in the melted chocolate to coat. Let the chocolate covering set before serving. Serve at room temperature.

Lobster and Foie Gras Balls

Makes 4 to 6 servings

2 eggs

2 cups **Dashi** (page 256)

1 tablespoon milk

2 cups all-purpose flour

1 tablespoon vegetable oil

4 ounces (100 g) cooked lobster, cut into ⅜-inch (2 cm) chunks

3 tablespoons finely chopped scallions

3 tablespoons finely chopped red pickled ginger

¼ cup *tonkatsu* sauce or *takoyaki* sauce (both available in Asian specialty stores)

In Japan, *takoyaki*, or octopus balls, are a popular street snack. Of course, to turn these into a Morimoto dish, I had to use lobster—and sometimes foie gras—in the center, rather than the humble octopus. This simple recipe is a puffed pancake cooked in a special pan, with curved indentations. These cast-iron pans are not expensive, and if you buy one, you can do more than contemplate this recipe, you can sample it. You could substitute cooked shrimp for the lobster.

1. In a large bowl, beat the eggs lightly. Whisk in the Dashi and milk. Add the flour and mix well to form a batter. Transfer to a 4-cup measure or batter bowl, if you have one.

2. Oil a traditional *takoyaki* pan, or a cast-iron, mini-muffin pan, and place over medium heat. Set small dishes with the lobster, scallions, and pickled ginger next to the stove.

3. When the pan is hot, pour enough batter into each small cup of the *takoyaki* pan to fill halfway. Put a chunk of lobster and a pinch of scallion and pickled ginger in the center of each. Pour in more batter to fill the cups to their rims.

4. Cook for 2 to 3 minutes, until the outside is nicely browned and crisp. Using a bamboo skewer, turn each ball upside down in the pan and cook for another 1 to 2 minutes to brown the second side.

5. Serve immediately, with *tonkatsu* or *takoyaki* sauce for dipping.

Blowfish Carpaccio

with Monkfish Liver-Ponzu Sauce

Makes 4 servings

While another mild white fish, like fluke, can be substituted here, it is a dish I usually make with blowfish (*fugu*). This is a delicacy, because only licensed chefs can prepare the *fugu*, which is potentially deadly if not properly butchered. I serve what is essentially blowfish sashimi with a pungent sauce that combines monkfish liver with tart Ponzu Sauce.

4 ounces (100 g) blowfish fillet or another sashimi-quality fine white fish, such as fluke or red snapper

3 tablespoons Monkfish Liver-Ponzu Sauce

¼ cup extra virgin olive oil

2 tablespoons baby cilantro leaves

2 tablespoons shaved white truffle or 1 tablespoon white truffle oil

....

MONKFISH LIVER-PONZU SAUCE
Makes about ⅓ cup

¼ cup Monkfish Liver Pâté

2 tablespoons Ponzu Sauce (page 260)

1 teaspoon soy sauce

Salt

....

MONKFISH LIVER PÂTÉ
Makes 1 pound (450 g)

1 pound (450 g) fresh monkfish liver

2 tablespoons salt

1 cup sake

1. Slice the fish fillet very thinly (see *usuzukuri* on page 21) and arrange on a heatproof plate. Drizzle the Monkfish Liver-Ponzu Sauce over the fish.

2. In a small saucepan, heat the olive oil until it just begins to smoke. Quickly and carefully, pour the hot oil over the fish slices to sear them.

3. Garnish with cilantro leaves and shaved white truffle or a drizzle of truffle oil.

Monkfish Liver-Ponzu Sauce

Blend together the Monkfish Liver Pâté, ponzu sauce, and soy sauce. Season with salt to taste.

Monkfish Liver Pâté

We butcher our own fish, but you can go to a high-quality fish monger and special-order the monkfish liver, so you don't have to remove it from the fish yourself.

1. Put the monkfish liver in a bowl, salt all over, and pour in the sake. Marinate in the refrigerator for 1 hour, turning the liver once.

2. Rinse the liver to remove the salt and sake. Clean it, removing all blood vessels.

3. Steam the liver for 25 minutes. Refrigerate until chilled. This can also be stored in a refriegerator for up to 3 days.

Parchment-wrapped Sea Bass

Makes 4 servings

I created this recipe especially for the holiday season, as the white and red string and nonedible holly garnish indicate. It's a simple method of rolling a sea bass in salt, wrapping it in Japanese rice paper, and baking it for 20 to 30 minutes. Obviously this would be tricky for you to recreate at home as the paper would burn, so I don't recommend it. However, the grilled fish, even without the paper, is delicious.

2 pound (900 g) sea bass

2 teaspoons salt

Japanese rice paper

Slices of lime, for garnish

1. Gut and clean the sea bass, leaving the head in place. Rub each side of the fish with 1 teaspoon of salt. Let sit on a large platter for 15 minutes.

2. Preheat the broiler. Grill the fish 4 inches (10 cm) from the heat for 2 minutes on each side.

3. Wrap the fish in rice paper, as shown in photograph, and place on a baking sheet. Lower the oven temperature to 250ºF (120ºC) and bake for 20 to 30 minutes.

4. To eat, unwrap the fish from the rice paper and serve with slices of lime.

Appetizers with 10 Tastes

This extravagant display is typical for special occasions. The customer can request special ingredients and note preferences, but it is up to the chef to choose the best fish according to availability and to use his creativity to contrast colors, flavors, and textures.

TOP ROW, FROM LEFT: **Shrimp and Egg Yolk Vinegar, Salted** *Uni* **in a** *Sudachi* **Cup,** *Karasumi* **and Daikon, Salmon and Fluke–Ball Sushi, and Egg Castella.**

BOTTOM ROW, FROM LEFT: **Monkfish Liver Pâté with Grated Daikon and Ponzu Sauce in a** *Yuzu* **Cup, Roasted Wagyu Beef, Salmon Roe in a** *Sudachi* **Cup, Japanese Tilefish** *Saikyo***, and** *Kohada Bo Zushi***.**

Squid Strawberry Ice Candy

Makes 4 servings

As you might guess, this is one of the recipes that I created in my guise as Iron Chef, turning a savory squid into a surprisingly delicate, sweet dessert.

½ pound (225 g) cleaned fresh squid fillets, no tentacles

1 egg white

1 cup Simple Syrup

4 strawberries

¼ cup raspberry liquor, such as Chambord or framboise

....

SIMPLE SYRUP

Makes about 1 cup

¾ cup sugar

¾ cup water

1. Purée the squid in a food processor. Add the egg white and Simple Syrup.

2. Fill a CO_2 canister with the squid mixture. Mound 3 tablespoons of the squid mixture in the center of a 6-inch (15 cm) square of plastic wrap. Pull the sides up and insert the strawberry into the center. Then completely wrap the strawberry in the squid by twisting the plastic wrap and forming a ball. Twst the ends to seal. Repeat to make 4 desserts.

3. Freeze the Squid Strawberry Ice Candy until solid. Cut each in half and serve in a small dish, with 1 tablespoon raspberry liqueur poured over as a sauce.

Simple Syrup

A staple of the dessert kitchen, Simple Syrup is 1 part sugar dissolved in 1 part water. Aside from its use in meringues and sorbets, it is good for sweetening cold drinks, like lemonade. The Simple Syrup will keep for months in the refrigerator in a covered jar. This recipe doubles easily.

In a small saucepan, combine the sugar and water. Bring to a boil over medium-high heat, stirring to dissolve the sugar. Remove from the heat. Use immediately or let cool, then refrigerate in a covered jar.

Vanilla Ice Cream
with Lobster Sauce

Makes 4 servings

1 cup whole milk

½ cup heavy cream

2 tablespoons sugar

½ vanilla bean, split
lengthwise in half

2 egg yolks

Lobster Sauce

....

LOBSTER SAUCE
Makes about 6 tablespoons

A long, slow reduction is key
to the success of this dish.
Be sure you use a heavy pan
and stir often, scraping down
the sides of the pan as well,
especially when the sauce
thickens, so that it does not
scorch.

2 pounds (900 g) lobster heads

3½ tablespoons vegetable oil

1 tablespoon brandy

1 tablespoon sake

1 onion, chopped

1 carrot, chopped

3 celery ribs, chopped

3 garlic cloves, chopped

⅓ cup tomato paste

3 sprigs of fresh thyme

3 bay leaves

1 tablespoon white
peppercorns

You will be surprised at how well the slightly bitter yet lightly sweet lobster sauce goes with vanilla ice cream. The caramelization of the protein in the lobster shells and the sugar in the tomato paste is accentuated during the long, slow reduction. Another creation for an "Iron Chef" battle, this is also a delicious ice cream to serve with chocolate or raspberry sauce.

1. In a small, heavy saucepan, heat the milk, heavy cream, sugar, and vanilla bean over medium heat, stirring to dissolve the sugar. Cook until bubbles appear around the rim of the pan.

2. In a small bowl, whisk the egg yolks to blend them. Gradually whisk in ½ cup of the hot milk to warm the eggs. Whisk the mixture into the remaining vanilla milk in the pan, reduce the heat to low, and cook, whisking until the custard is thick enough to coat the back of a spoon, 180°F (80°C).

3. Strain through a fine sieve into a heatproof bowl. Set over a bowl of ice and water and stir until cooled. Then cover and refrigerate until chilled, at least 2 hours.

4. Turn the vanilla custard into an ice cream maker and freeze according to the manufacturer's instructions. Transfer the ice cream to a covered container and freeze for at least 3 hours, or overnight, until the ice cream is firm enough to scoop.

5. Serve the ice cream with a drizzle of the thick lobster sauce.

Lobster Sauce

1. In a sauté pan, sear the lobster heads over high heat in 1½ tablespoons of the oil until they turn red, about 3 minutes. Pour in the brandy and sake, toss, and remove from the heat.

2. In a large saucepan, sauté the onion, carrot, celery, and garlic in the remaining oil over medium-high heat until softened but not browned, 3 to 5 minutes.

3. Add the sautéed lobster heads with any juices in the pan, the tomato paste, thyme, bay leaves, white peppercorns, and enough water to cover, about 4 cups. Bring to a boil, skimming off any scum that rises to the surface. Reduce the heat and simmer for 1 hour, adding water if needed to keep the ingredients covered.

4. Strain the lobster stock through a fine sieve. Return to a small heavy saucepan and simmer over low heat, stirring often to avoid scorching, until the sauce is thick and reduced to about 6 tablespoons.

Desserts

Red Miso Soufflé

Makes 4 servings

Red miso makes a soufflé that is buttery yet has a unique kick. This is especially delicious served with softened Yuzu Ice Cream (see page 252) as a sauce.

2 teaspoons unsalted butter

½ cup red miso

1¼ cups sugar

6 whole eggs, separated

6 egg whites

1. Preheat the oven to 375°F (190°C). Butter 4 (8-ounce /225 g) ramekins or individual soufflé dishes.

2. In a large mixing bowl, whisk together the red miso, ¼ cup of the sugar, and the 6 egg yolks. Blend well.

3. In another large mixing bowl, beat the 12 egg whites until frothy. Gradually add the remaining 1 cup of sugar while continuing to beat until soft peaks form. Fold the beaten whites into the red miso base. Divide among the ramekins. Level off the tops with a spatula.

4. Bake for 8 to 10 minutes, until puffed and just set. Serve immediately.

Sweet Potato Cake

with Red Bean Foam

Makes 8 servings

Rich and only mildly sweet, this is more of a baked pudding than a cake. While the photo at left shows the dessert prepared in a sweet potato shell, we usually cook it in a baking pan and serve it in squares with a Red Bean Foam "frosting," so it looks like a pastry.

2 cups Japanese sweet potato purée (made from 3 medium roasted and puréed *satsu-maimo*, though regular sweet potatoes can be substituted)

4 whole eggs

¼ cup sugar

¾ cup unsalted butter (1½ sticks), kneaded until soft

8 egg yolks

4 tablespoons condensed milk

¼ cup honey

2 teaspoons baking powder

....

RED BEAN FOAM

¼ cup milk

¼ cup sweet red bean paste

¼ cup heavy cream

1. Preheat the oven to 325°F (160°C). Bake the potatoes until they are completely soft, about 1 hour. As soon as they are cool enough to handle, split in half and scoop the potato into a bowl. Purée in a food processor until creamy and smooth.

2. In a mixer bowl, beat the whole eggs and sugar until well combined. Scrape into a small bowl and set aside.

3. In the mixer bowl, use the paddle attachment to beat together the butter and the sweet potato purée until smooth. Alternatively, use an electric hand mixer. Beat in the egg yolks. Fold in the beaten whole eggs and sugar. Mix in the honey and condensed milk, then the baking powder.

4. Turn the batter into an unbuttered 8-inch (20 cm) square baking pan. Bake for about 20 minutes at 325°F (160°C). The cake is set when a skewer inserted in the middle comes out clean. Let cool in the pan for 20 minutes before unmolding the cake. The cake should be served at room temperature.

Red Bean Foam

1. Whisk the milk, red bean paste, and heavy cream together. Push the mixture through a mesh strainer to remove the bean skins.

2. Whip with a hand blender until soft peaks are formed. Spoon over the cake.

Tofu Cheesecake with Coffee-Infused Maple Syrup

Makes 6 servings

While this light and creamy dessert makes a visual pun on savory tofu, which it resembles, it is actually made with fresh soy milk. Squares of the cheesecake "tofu" are garnished with dark green, minced Candied Lime Zest that resembles minced chives, a drizzle of Coffee-Infused Maple Syrup as dark as soy sauce, and Candied Yuba. It may look like a main dish, but it satisfies as only dessert can. For an easier though less witty home presentation, fresh berries pair well with the cheesecake.

⅓ cup heavy cream

2 large egg whites

⅓ cup plus 2 tablespoons sugar

4 ounces (100 g) cream cheese

½ cup fresh soy milk

½ packet (1¼ teaspoons) gelatin softened in 1 tablespoon cold water

Candied Lime Zest
(recipe follows)

Coffee-Infused Maple Syrup
(recipe follows)

Candied Yuba
(recipe follows)

1. In a medium bowl, beat the cream with an electric mixer until stiff. Transfer to a small bowl, cover and refrigerate.

2. In a heatproof mixing bowl, beat the egg whites with 2 tablespoons of the sugar until soft peaks form. Set aside.

3. In a small saucepan, combine the remaining ⅓ cup sugar with 3 tablespoons of water. Bring to a boil, stirring to dissolve the sugar. Boil without stirring until the syrup reaches the soft-ball stage, 235° to 240°F (115°C). Gradually beat the hot syrup into the whipped egg whites. Continue to beat until the meringue is cool and very stiff.

4. In a stainless steel bowl or double boiler, blend the cream cheese and fresh soy milk and gently heat over simmering water, stirring, until it is warm. Stir in the softened gelatin and continue to cook, stirring, for 1 minute to make sure all the gelatin is dissolved.

5. Fold the cream cheese mixture into the meringue. Next fold in the whipped cream. Turn into a 6-inch (15 cm) square pan. Flip it over onto a sheet pan or platter. Refrigerate for at least 2 hours, or overnight.

6. To serve, unmold and cut the cheesecake into 2-inch (5 cm) squares. Drizzle the Candied Lime Zest and Coffee-Infused Maple Syrup on the side of each square, and place the Candied Yuba on top.

continued . . .

Tofu Cheesecake with
Coffee-Infused Maple Syrup continued

Candied Lime Zest

Makes about 1 tablespoon

2 limes

1 cup water

1 cup sugar

1. With a zester, remove the outer dark-green peel of the limes in thin strips.

2. Put the lime zest in a small saucepan, fill it with water, and bring to a boil; drain. Repeat this process 2 more times to remove any trace of bitterness. After the last draining, rinse the zest under cold running water to stop the cooking.

3. In a clean, small saucepan, combine the sugar and water. Bring to a boil, stirring to dissolve the sugar. Add the lime zest, reduce the heat to a simmer, and cook for 30 minutes.

4. Remove from the heat and let the candied zest cool in the syrup. Before using, strain and cut the strips into small dice to resemble minced chives.

Coffee-Infused Maple Syrup

Makes 2/3 cup

2 tablespoons instant coffee

2 tablespoons hot water

½ cup maple syrup

1 tablespoon sugar

In a small saucepan, dissolve the coffee in the hot water. Add the maple syrup and sugar and bring to a boil over medium heat, stirring occasionally. Remove from the heat and let cool. Cover and chill before serving.

Candied Yuba

Makes 6 candies

Yuba comes two ways, fresh and and dried. Fresh is made from skimming simmering soy milk. Dried can be purchased from an Asian specialty store.

1 cup water

1 cup sugar

1 sheet of dried *yuba*

1. Boil the sugar and water in a small saucepan over medium-high heat, stirring to dissolve the sugar, until it forms a light syrup. Remove from the heat and cool.

2. Brush the yuba with the syrup and set aside until the syrup dries.

3. Dust with powdered sugar and break into pieces for garnish.

Sugared Salmon

with Beet Sorbet and Yuzu Foam

Makes 4 servings

4 ounces (100 g) salmon fillet

2 teaspoons salt

⅓ cup brandy

½ cup Demerara sugar
(raw granulated brown sugar)

1 teaspoon freshly ground
black pepper

2 star anise pods, cracked
into pieces

2 or 3 cinnamon sticks, broken
in half

Beet Sorbet (recipe follows)

Yuzu Foam (page 260)

4 fresh mint leaves or small
sprigs of mint

You might be tempted to serve this as a first course, but trust me, it is definitely a dessert, though one that will play tricks on your senses. What is normally savory is made sweet and flavored with sweet spices. There are also some wonderful textures at play, with the gossamer salmon and icy beet sorbet.

1. Holding your knife on an angle, cut the salmon into 8 to 12 very thin slices **(photo 02, on page 241)**. Lay out the salmon slices on a large plate or tray and sprinkle them with the salt **(photos 03 and 04)**. Rinse under running water, then return to plate and cover with a towel to absorb the liquid that is exuded **(photo 05)**.

2. Put the brandy in a small bowl, dip the salmon slices in the brandy, and let sit for 15 minutes **(photo 06)**. Cover a dish large enough to hold the salmon with half the sugar. Arrange the slices in a single layer **(photo 07)**.

3. Combine the remaining brown sugar with the black pepper, star anise, and cinnamon sticks and sprinkle over the salmon **(photos 08 and 09)**.

4. Cover with plastic wrap and refrigerate for 30 minutes.

5. To serve, wipe the sugar and spice coating off the salmon. Arrange 2 or 3 pieces of the sugared salmon on each plate. Add a scoop of beet sorbet. Decorate the plate, if you like, with Yuzu Foam and garnish with fresh mint leaves.
continued . . .

Beet Sorbet

Makes 1 pound (450 g)

**½ pound (225 g) beets, trimmed,
peeled and quartered**

**3 sheets (2 g each) of
unflavored gelatin**

**¾ cup plus 2 tablespoons
granulated sugar**

1. Boil the beets in a saucepan of water until they are very
tender, about 30 to 40 minutes; drain, reserving ¼ cup of
the cooking water. Transfer the beets to a blender or food
processor and purée; add 3 to 4 tablespoons of the beet
cooking water, if necessary, to make a smooth purée.

2. Sprinkle the gelatin over 2 tablespoons cold water and
let stand until softened, 5 to 10 minutes.

3. Meanwhile, transfer the beet purée to a nonreactive
medium saucepan. Add the sugar and 2 cups of water.
Slowly bring to a boil over medium heat, skimming off any
scum that rises to the top and stirring to dissolve the sugar.
As soon as the mixture begins to boil, remove from the
heat and stir in the softened gelatin.

4. Let the beet mixture cool for 10 minutes. Strain through
a fine sieve and let cool slightly, then cover and refrigerate
until completely chilled, at least 3 hours or overnight.

5. Pour the beet mixture into the canister of an ice cream
machine and freeze according to the manufacturer's
instructions. Transfer to a covered container and freeze until
firm enough to scoop, at least 4 hours.

01

02

03

04

05

06

07

08

09

241

Desserts

Sake

Some people take sake too seriously, speaking about it in the hushed tones usually reserved for making big business deals. Drinking it is supposed to be fun. Of course, that's not to say that sake, often referred to as "Japanese rice wine," isn't seriously delicious. Its flavors are as complex and nuanced as those in great wine or beer. I drink it with everything, including foie gras. And because it's made from rice, it occupies a special place in Japanese culture: sake plays a role in Japanese rites of cleansing, purification, and even in the marriage ceremony. At weddings, for instance, couples symbolize their union by drinking sake from the same cup.

The magic of sake is that the alcoholic beverage brewed from just rice and water can provide an endless spectrum of flavors and aromas, such as peaches, pears, bananas, melons, flowers, and grass. Fine sake is not to be guzzled but savored. Before I taste or even smell it, I like to admire its color. It might be crystal clear, faintly gold, or even milky white. Then, I dip my nose in the glass, just above the liquid. I take in the aroma—crisp and clean, tinged with fruit and minerals. Finally, it's time to taste. You won't have to search for the flavor: It'll explode in your mouth, sending out lush sweetness, bracing acidity, and complex mineral notes in all directions before it slowly fades from your palate.

Sake is grouped into two broad categories: *junmai* (sake made from just rice and water) and *honjozo* (sake made with rice and distilled alcohol). Within these groupings, the drink is categorized by how much the rice is polished. Sakes brewed from grains of rice that have been milled until no more than 50 percent of each grain remains are called *dai ginjo*. These are generally full-bodied and fragrant with subtle, refined flavors. I love to drink these alone or with light food. *Ginjo* refers to sake made from grains polished to no more than 60 percent of their initial size. Sakes within this category tend to be light and highly aromatic, with a quiet elegance similar to that of *dai ginjo*. Until recently, those labeled *junmai* had to be made from rice polished until no more than 70 percent of each grain remains. Now, more than 70 percent of the rice can remain, so long as the percentage of rice milled away appears somewhere on the label. Because of their more assertive flavor and sprightly acidity, *junmai* are my favorite sakes to drink with food. At my restaurants, I serve sake made especially for me by Fukumitsuya, a brewery in Kanazawa, Japan, dating back to 1625.

The sake-making process is a complex one. Rice must be polished, then steamed before being inoculated with *Aspergillus oryzae* mold, or *koji* in Japanese. Next, it is transferred to a warm, humid room whose conditions are constantly monitored, for they are essential to the proper development of the mold. (There is now a great deal of research on *koji* going on in Japan, as brewers seek to develop new strains of the mold, particularly those that grow on fruit, to produce new flavors of sake.) When *koji*, which looks like pale-yellow powder, is evenly distributed and then massaged into the rice, it's nearly invisible. But after a couple of days, it becomes a noticeable fuzzy layer. If all goes well, the *koji* multiplies at a fast pace, turning some of the starches in the rice to sugars. This rice is then combined with plain steamed rice, a yeast starter, and springwater. As water makes up nearly 80 percent of the final product, its quality and mineral composition are a big part of determining the sake's personality.

OPPOSITE PAGE: **These two bottles are Morimoto aged sakes—the one at left is 10 years old and the one at right is 30 years old.**

TOP LEFT: **This is a Morimoto *junmai* sake, made from just rice and water.**

TOP RIGHT: **All the sake carafes and glasses at Morimoto New York were made especially for my restaurant. The glasses have inadvertently become "souvenirs" for customers.**

It takes a minimum of two weeks and sometimes much longer for this mixture of rice, water, and yeast to develop properly. When the conditions are ready for the final fermentation, more steamed rice and water are added, and the process begins in giant vats. Yeast is a living thing, a tiny voracious organism that is nearly as unpredictable as we are. Therefore, a sake brewer must carefully observe the vats as the yeast converts sugars to alcohol and carbon dioxide, watching and listening to the foamy bubbles that form on top of the liquid. These sights and sounds tell him whether the fermentation is happening at the appropriate speed and whether he must adjust by, for example, changing the liquid's temperature. Finally, when the brewer has decided his brew is ready, he strains off the liquid. Often, it is filtered to purge it of unwanted colors and flavors; sometimes, however, it isn't, which results in a cloudy, delicious kind of sake called *nigori*. Then, it's pasteurized, typically twice, though again, a brewer may choose not to do so at all. Unpasteurized sake is called *nama*.

When sake is used in cooking, the alcohol is often boiled off and a delectable sweetness from the rice remains. It's added to marinades, boiled with soy sauce, used as a steaming liquid, and much more. Keep in mind, though, that the famous wine adage, "Don't cook with it if you wouldn't drink it," applies to sake as well.

Chocolate Tart with White Chocolate Sorbet

Makes 6 to 8 servings

1 cup heavy cream

1 tablespoon corn syrup

1 pinch salt

½ cup sugar

2 tablespoons water

1 tablespoon unsalted butter

13 ounces (375 g) bittersweet dark chocolate 70%, finely chopped

3 ounces (75 g) milk chocolate, finely chopped

TART DOUGH

Makes 6 to 8 tarts

8 tablespoons unsalted butter, cold

½ cup sugar

1 pinch salt

1 tablespoon almond flour

2 egg yolks

1 tablespoon cocoa powder

1 cup all-purpose flour

WHITE CHOCOLATE SORBET

Makes about 1½ pints (675 ml)

1 cup water

1 cup plus 2 tablespoons sugar

2 tablespoons light corn syrup

8 ounces (225 g) white chocolate, coarsely chopped

Guests are surprised when they spoon up what they think is vanilla ice cream and discover instead this hedonistic, dairy-free White Chocolate Sorbet. It's wonderful in a goblet, with a drizzle of raspberry or dark chocolate sauce. At the restaurant, we pair it with our intense bittersweet Chocolate Tart.

1. Combine the heavy cream, corn syrup, and salt in a saucepan and bring to a boil. Turn off the heat.

2. In a separate pot, dissolve the sugar into the water and bring to a boil over medium-high heat. Lower to medium-low and let boil for 5 to 7 minutes, until a light caramel color is achieved. Add butter and melt into the caramel.

3. Off the heat, pour the warm heavy cream mixture into the caramel. Stir in the chocolate until melted and thoroughly combined.

5. Pour the mixture into a 9-inch (22 cm) tart pan and refrigerate at least 2 hours until set.

Tart Dough

1. Cut the butter, sugar, and salt together in a large bowl.

2. Stir in the almond flour and egg yolks.

3. Sift cocoa powder and all purpose flour together, then add to the butter and knead just enough to form into a ball. Flatten the dough into a disc, wrap in plastic wrap, and chill for 2 hours.

4. Preheat the oven to 350°F (180°C).

5. On a lightly floured surface, roll out the dough to a thickness of ⅛ inch (3 cm). Pierce the dough all over with a fork. Cut into squares about 2½ inches (6 cm) on a side.

6. Bake the tarts on a lightly floured baking sheet for 15 minutes, until lightly browned.

7. Pour the chocolate filling into the tart shell and serve immediately with a scoop of the White Chocolate Sorbet.

White Chocolate Sorbet

1. In a medium saucepan, combine the water, sugar, and corn syrup. Bring to a boil, stirring to dissolve the sugar. Remove from the heat and add the white chocolate. Let stand for 30 seconds, then whisk until smooth.

2. Let the sorbet base cool to room temperature. Whisk again and turn into an ice cream machine. Process according to the manufacturer's instructions; it will be softly frozen. Transfer to a covered container and freeze for at least 4 hours or overnight until firm.

Kabosu Crème Brûlée

Makes 4 servings

Crème brûlée is extremely popular these days. I wanted to have it on my menu, but as usual, I wanted to tie it into my own cuisine. I've flavored it with *kabosu*, a Japanese citrus fruit that looks like a small green orange and has the flavor not unlike a lemon.

6 egg yolks

¾ cup sugar

½ cup milk

½ cup heavy cream

¼ cup *kabosu* juice (available in Asian specialty stores)

Slivered *kabosu* zest, for garnish

1. In a medium bowl, whisk the egg yolks lightly. Gradually beat in ½ cup of the sugar and continue to beat until the mixture lightens and forms a ribbon when the beaters are lifted, about 2 minutes.

2. Heat the milk until bubbles appear around the edge of pan then remove from heat. Gradually whisk the warmed milk into the yolks. Strain into a bowl.

3. Whisk in the heavy cream. Let cool slightly, then cover and let cool completely, about 2 hours. Stir in the *kabosu* juice.

4. Preheat the oven to 200°F (90°C). Divide the custard among 4 heatproof shallow (8-ounce/225 g) custard cups. Set them on a sheet pan and bake until set, about 1 hour. Set aside to cool. Cover and refrigerate until chilled, 3 hours or overnight.

5. Before serving, sprinkle 1 tablespoon of the remaining sugar over each dish. Caramelize with a blowtorch or under a hot broiler. Garnish with the *kabosu* zest and serve immediately.

Raspberry Tofu Vacherin

Makes 6 servings

Here I take a classic French meringue-based dessert, *vacherin*, which is traditionally formed in a mold and both deconstruct it and give it a subtle Asian twist with sesame seeds, soy milk, and *yuzu*. The dessert is assembled freeform from three components, all of which should be made in advance.

Sesame Meringue

Tofu Ice Cream

Raspberry Yuzu Foam

²/₃ cup fresh raspberries

6 sprigs of mint

··

SESAME MERINGUE

Makes about 30

2 large egg whites

1 cup sugar

¹/₃ cup sesame seeds

3 tablespoons all-purpose flour

··

TOFU ICE CREAM

Makes 1 quart (1 liter)

4 egg yolks

¾ cup sugar

2 cups fresh soy milk

1 cup heavy cream

··

RASPBERRY YUZU FOAM

Makes 1½ cups

**1 cup raspberry purée
(¾ cup raspberries;
2 tablespoons sugar)**

**½ packet gelatin (¹/₈ ounce/
3 g), softened in 1 tablespoon
cold water for 3 to 5 minutes**

¼ cup *yuzu*, or lemon juice

1.   Make the Sesame Meringue up to 3 days in advance. Make the Tofu Ice Cream at least 6 hours or up to a day in advance. Make the base for the foam up to a day in advance.

2.   For each serving, place a scoop or two of Tofu Ice Cream on a plate. Add 5 or 6 raspberries and scoop out a large dollop of Raspberry Yuzu Foam. Top with 2 or 3 Sesame Meringues and garnish with a sprig of mint.

Sesame Meringue

1.   Preheat the oven to 300°F (150°C).

2.   Whisk the egg whites and sugar in a double boiler or in a stainless steel bowl over a pan of simmering water until the mixture is warm and the sugar is dissolved.

3.   Beat until the meringue is cooled and the whites form stiff peaks. Combine the sesame seeds and flour, then stir into the beaten egg whites just until combined.

4.   Transfer the sesame meringue to a pastry bag fitted with a ½-inch (12 mm) plain tip. Holding the tip of the pastry bag close to a sheet pan lined with a silicone mat or parchment paper, pipe out about 30 (3-inch/7 cm long) sticks.

5.   Bake until dry but not colored, about 10 to 15 minutes. Let cool completely before storing in an airtight container.

Tofu Ice Cream

1.   In a heatproof bowl, whisk the egg yolks to break them up. Gradually whisk in the sugar and continue beating until the mixture is thick and pale.

2.   In a heavy, medium saucepan, heat the soy milk gently until bubbles appear around the edge of the pan. Slowly beat the hot milk into the yolks. Return all the mixture to the saucepan and cook over medium-low heat, stirring constantly, until the custard is thick enough to coat the back of a spoon. Strain into a bowl and let cool slightly, then cover and refrigerate until chilled.*

3.   Stir in the heavy cream. Turn into the canister of an ice cream machine and freeze according to the manufacturer's instructions. Transfer the frozen soy milk to a covered container and freeze until hard enough to scoop, at least 4 hours or overnight.

*You can speed this up by setting the bowl of custard into a larger bowl filled with ice and water and stirring until cold.

Raspberry Yuzu Foam

1.   Gently heat the raspberry purée in a saucepan until warm to the touch. Transfer the purée to a small nonreactive saucepan and warm over medium-low heat. Scrape the softened gelatin into the purée and simmer for 2 minutes, stirring, until the gelatin is dissolved.

2.   Remove from the heat and stir in the *yuzu* juice. Let cool completely, then cover and refrigerate for at least 2 hours or overnight, until cold. To use, whip with a hand blender until soft peaks are formed.

Asparagus Pocky

Makes 4 to 6 servings

In Japan, they sell long, thin cigarette-shaped cookies coated with chocolate, which are called *pocky*. They're very popular just to nibble as a sweet snack or as a garnish to a frozen dessert. This is my surprise version of them, made with a vegetable instead of a cookie. Fans of "Iron Chef" will understand how such a treatment might evolve. While you could make the *pocky* with any asparagus, white is milder and more appropriate for this dish.

    Note: Couverture chocolate is a high-quality chocolate rich in cocoa butter. It is excellent for coating, because after being "tempered" (see Step 3), it dries to a thin, crisp, glossy shell. A pound is lot, but you'll need at least that much in order to be able to dip the asparagus. Use any leftover to coat strawberries, dried apricots, or plain cookies.

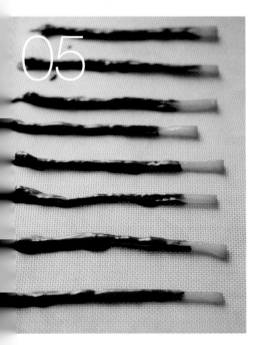

12 thin white asparagus spears (about 1 pound/450 g)

2 cups plum wine

3½ tablespoons brandy

3½ tablespoons Sprite soda

1 tablespoon grated *yuzu,* or lemon zest

1 cinnamon stick

4 star anise pods

1 teaspoon black peppercorns

Splash of light-colored soy sauce

1 pound (450 g) bittersweet chocolate, preferably bittersweet couverture, coarsely chopped

1. Using a swivel-blade vegetable peeler, remove the outside peel from the asparagus. If the spears are not very thin, continue to peel all around, leaving the tips untouched, until the stems are reduced to ⅜ inch (9 mm) in diameter **(photo 01)**. Set aside on a plate, covered with a damp towel.

2. Prepare the infusion for the asparagus in a pressure cooker: Combine the asparagus, plum wine, brandy, Sprite, *yuzu* zest, cinnamon, star anis, black peppercorns, and soy sauce and heat until the cooker whistles. Reduce heat and continue to cook for 30 minutes. Alternatively, combine the same ingredients in a nonreactive medium saucepan **(photos 02 and 03)**. Bring to a simmer, reduce heat to low, and cook for 90 minutes. Remove from the heat, cover, and let steep for 30 minutes.

3. In a double boiler, or a metal bowl set over a pan of simmering water, melt the chocolate very carefully; do not let the bottom of the bowl touch the water. Heat ¾ of the chocolate to 110° to 115°F (45°C), not more; use a candy thermometer or digital instant read to measure exactly.

4. Remove from the heat, add the remaining chocolate, and stir until smooth and melted. Finally, heat the chocolate again very slowly, stirring, until it reaches 90°F (30°C).

5. Holding the asparagus by the end of the stem, dip in the melted chocolate to coat **(photo 04)**. Hold until set, then place on a tray lined with waxed paper **(photo 05)**. Repeat to coat all the spears. Set aside until the coating hardens to a glossy shell. Refrigerate for longer storage.

Yuzu Ice Cream

Makes about 1 pint

This ice cream is subtly flavored with *yuzu*, a citrus fruit favored by not only Japanese chefs, but by chefs everywhere who get to sample its inimitable taste. The juice can be had from the fresh fruit or is sold jarred or frozen in Asian specialty stores. When *yuzu* is not available, though, fresh lemon juice can be substituted.

2 large egg yolks

½ cup sugar

1 cup milk

½ cup heavy cream

¼ cup *yuzu* juice

1. In a heatproof medium bowl, beat the egg yolks lightly. Gradually whisk in the sugar and beat until the mixture is thick and pale, about 2 minutes.

2. In a small saucepan, heat the milk until bubbles appear around the rim of the pan. Gradually whisk about ⅓ cup of the hot milk into the yolks to warm them. Slowly whisk the yolks back into the remaining milk in the pan.

3. Reduce the heat to low and cook, stirring, until the custard is thick enough to coat the back of a spoon. Strain into a clean bowl, set over a larger bowl of ice and water and stir until cooled.

4. Whisk in the heavy cream and *yuzu* juice. Cover and refrigerate for 1 to 2 hours, until chilled.

5. Pour into the canister of an ice cream machine and process according to the manufacturer's instructions. Transfer to a covered container and freeze for at least 3 hours, or overnight, until firm enough to scoop.

Stocks, Oils, Spices, and Sauces

Shanton Broth

Makes 3 quarts (3 liters)

This clear golden liquid is the all-purpose meat stock used in my kitchens. Instead of utilizing just one meat, I combine chicken, pork, and beef for a stock with depth of taste and supple body. Another interesting change from a classic French stock is the lack of vegetables—the stock is seasoned with dried *longan*, for the barest hint of sweetness, as well as with dried citrus, and white peppercorns.

1½ pounds (675 g) fresh ham, trimmed of fat and sinew, cut into 1½-inch (4 cm) pieces

1 pound (450 g) chicken thighs or drumsticks, chopped into large pieces with a cleaver

1 pound (450 g) pork neck bones

1 pound (450 g) beef shin

2 teaspoons dried *longan*

2 pieces dried citrus peel, about 1-inch (2½ cm) square each

8 white peppercorns

1. Bring a large stockpot of water to a boil over high heat. Have a large bowl of ice water nearby.

2. Add the ham and cook until the water comes back to a boil. Using a large wire skimmer or slotted spoon, transfer the ham to the ice water to cool down immediately. Remove the blanched ham from the ice water and drain in a large colander.

3. In separate batches, repeat the blanching and shocking in ice water with the chicken, pork neck bones, and beef shin. (Two pots of boiling water come in handy here to speed up the process.) This step removes blood and excess fat from the meat and helps create a clear stock.

4. Rinse the meat in the colander and clean the stockpot before returning the meat to the stockpot. Add fresh cold water to cover the meats by 1 inch (2½ cm). Bring to a boil over high heat, skimming off any foam that rises to the surface. Reduce the heat to low and simmer, skimming whenever needed, for 4 hours.

5. Add the *longan*, citrus peel, and peppercorns and continue simmering for 2 hours longer.

6. Strain the stock in a chinois or colander over a large bowl sitting in a larger bowl of ice water. Cool. Transfer the stock to covered containers. Refrigerate for up to 3 days, or freeze for up to 2 months.

Chicken Stock

Makes 3 to 4 quarts (3 to 4 liters)

Depending upon how much you reduce your stock, this will make 12 to 16 cups. It's more than you need for any one recipe, but stock freezes well, and it's always nice to have on hand for soups and stews.

3 to 4 pounds (1½ kg) chicken bones (backs, wings, and necks)

3 celery ribs, quartered

2 carrots, peeled and quartered

1 medium onion, quartered

8 parsley sprigs with stems

4 sprigs of thyme

1. Rinse the chicken well. Place in a large stockpot along with the celery, carrots, and onion. Add 6 to 8 quarts of cold water. Bring to a boil, skimming off all the foam that rises to the surface.

2. Add the parsley and thyme. Reduce the heat to low and cook for 5 to 6 hours, adding more water if necessary. Strain through a fine mesh sieve. If the stock has not reduced enough, pour into a clean large pot and boil until reduced to 3 or 4 quarts (3 to 4 liters).

Dashi

Makes 1 quart (1 liter)

This is the most common of all Japanese stocks, but it doesn't have to be mundane. There is a wide range of quality in *kombu* and bonito, and for the best dashi, you simply use the best ingredients. In fact, because dashi usually only has three components, I strongly believe that they must be of the highest quality, beginning with filtered water. Start the night before to soak the *kombu*, but do not make more dashi than you need, as it does not refrigerate or freeze well.

1 piece of dashi *kombu*, 4 x 6 inches (10 to 15 cm)

4 cups filtered springwater

½ cup loosely packed bonito flakes

1. The night before using the dashi, wipe the *kombu* clean with a wet kitchen towel to remove any grit, but do not rub off the white powder; much of the flavor lies in its natural MSG. Place in a medium saucepan and add the springwater. Let stand at room temperature overnight.

2. The next day, remove the *kombu* and bring the water to a simmer over medium heat. When it reaches a boil, remove from heat and add the *bonito* flakes. Let stand until the *bonito* flakes sink to the bottom of the saucepan, about 15 minutes.

3. Line a wire sieve with moistened, squeezed-dry cheesecloth and place over a bowl. Strain the dashi through the sieve. Use the dashi within a couple of hours of making.

Veal Stock

Makes about 3 quarts (3 liters)

All the roasted veal bones here give off lots of gelatin to create a lush stock with lots of body. I use it to add a firm meaty note to sauces. If you reduce the stock as suggested below, you'll end up with an intensely flavored liquid that can add tremendous depth of flavor to dishes. Veal Reduction is a close cousin to *glace de viande*, one of the ingredients that gives French food its elegance.

3 pounds (1 kg) veal bones

1 medium onion, chopped

1 medium carrot, chopped

1 medium celery rib, chopped

1 cup hearty red wine

1 tablespoon tomato paste

6 sprigs of fresh parsley

2 sprigs of fresh thyme

1 bay leaf

1. Preheat the oven to 425°F (220°C). Spread out the veal bones in a large half-sheet pan or shallow roasting pan. Roast, turning the bones occasionally, until they are well browned but not burned, about 40 minutes.

2. Transfer the roasted bones to a large stockpot. Pour off all but 2 tablespoons of the fat from the baking pan. Add the onion, carrot, and celery to the baking pan and stir to coat with the fat. Return to the oven and roast, stirring occasionally, until the vegetables are lightly browned, 15 to 20 minutes. Transfer the vegetables into the stockpot.

3. Set the baking pan over medium-high heat on the stovetop. Pour in the wine and bring to a boil, scraping up the browned bits from the bottom of the pan iwht a wooden spatula. Pour the liquid into the stockpot.

4. Add enough cold water to cover the veal and vegetables by 2 inches (5 cm), about 4 quarts (4 liters). Bring to a boil over high heat, skimming off any foam that rises to the surface. Add the tomato paste, parsley, thyme, and bay leaf. Reduce the heat to very low. Simmer the stock for at least 6 and up to 12 hours, adding more cold water as needed to keep the veal covered.

5. Strain the stock through a fine sieve into a large bowl. Let cool to room temperature. Skim off any clear fat from the surface. Transfer to covered containers and refrigerate for up to 3 days or freeze for up to 3 months.

Veal Reduction

Makes about ½ cup

1. Refrigerate 2 quarts (2 liters) of Veal Stock overnight.

2. Scrape off any solidified fat from the surface. Bring the stock to a boil over high heat in a medium saucepan. Boil until the stock is reduced to a syrupy consistency, about 1 hour, taking care at the end that you don't reduce the stock too much and scorch the reduction.

3. Cool slightly, then transfer to small covered containers. Refrigerate for up to 1 week, or freeze for up to 3 months.

Beef Stock

Makes about 3½ cups

1 beef shin, about 1 pound (450 g)

2 canned tomatoes, drained and chopped, or 1 tablespoon tomato paste

1 small onion, coarsely chopped

1 small carrot, coarsely chopped

1 small celery rib, coarsely chopped

2 garlic cloves, crushed

2 sprigs of fresh thyme

1 bay leaf

4 cups Veal Stock

1. Place the beef shin, tomatoes, onion, carrot, and celery in a heavy, medium saucepan. Pour in the Veal Stock and bring to a boil over high heat, skimming off any foam as it rises to the surface.

2. Add the garlic, thyme, and bay leaf. Reduce the heat to low, partially cover, and simmer, adding water as needed to maintain the liquid, for 2 to 3 hours. Strain through a sieve. Skim all the fat from the top. Measure 2 cups of the stock base and set aside. Reserve the remaining stock (it freezes well) for another use; it is great in any recipe that calls for veal or beef stock.

Lobster Broth

Makes about 4 cups

Some fish markets will sell lobster heads at a good price. If yours does not, opt for a couple of small lobsters. Culls, those with a missing or stunted claw, are fine for stock and are usually less expensive.

2 pounds (900 g) lobster heads

1½ tablespoons vegetable oil

1 tablespoon brandy

1 tablespoon sake

1 onion, chopped

1 carrot, chopped

3 celery ribs, chopped

3 garlic cloves, chopped

⅓ cup tomato paste

3 sprigs of fresh thyme

3 bay leaves

1 tablespoon white peppercorns

1.   In a sauté pan, sear the lobster heads over high heat in the vegetable oil until they turn red, about 3 minutes. Pour in the brandy and sake, toss, and remove from the heat.

2.   In a large side saucepan, sauté the onion, carrot, celery, garlic, and scallion in the remaining oil over medium-high heat until softened but not browned, 3 to 5 minutes.

3.   Add the sautéed lobster heads with any juices in the pan, the tomato paste, thyme, bay leaves, white peppercorns, and enough water to cover, about 4 cups. Bring to a boil, skimming off any scum that rises to the surface. Reduce the heat and simmer for 1 hour, adding water if needed to keep the ingredients covered. Strain the lobster broth through a fine sieve pressing on the solids to extract as much liquid as possible. Let cool, then cover and refrigerate for up to 3 days or freeze for up to 2 months.

Fish Fumet

Makes about 1½ quarts (1½ liters)

Because fish gives off its flavor so readily, fish stock, or fumet, is made much more quickly than meat stocks. In fact, so that it doesn't turn bitter, fumet, is rarely simmered for longer than 30 minutes. I add just a hint of chile pepper to punch up the fish's clean flavor. The most difficult part is finding a fishmonger who saves fish bones and heads for cooks who want to make fish fumet, but a Chinese or Italian fish market is a good place to start. You can also buy a fish or two and have them filleted—serve the filets for dinner and make the bones and heads into fumet. But be sure to use white-flesh fish, and skip oily ones like salmon, bluefish, or mackerel, which are too strong for stock.

1 pound (450 g) fish bones and/or heads

3 tablespoons coarse salt

2 tablespoons vegetable oil

½ fresh jalapeño pepper, cut into thin rounds, with seeds

1.   If the fish heads have gills, snip them out with scissors and discard them. Rinse the fish parts under cold running water. Place in a colander and sprinkle all over with the salt. Let stand for about 20 minutes. Rinse again.

2.   Transfer the bones to a large saucepan and add enough water to cover, about 2 quarts (2 liters). Bring to a boil over high heat, skimming off any foam that rises to the surface. Reduce the heat to low and simmer for 30 minutes. Strain the fumet.

3.   Heat the oil in another large saucepan until the oil begins to shimmer. Add the jalapeño and cook until the oil starts to smoke. Carefully pour in the fumet, as the liquid may splatter. Bring to a boil, then remove from the heat. Let cool; store in covered containers for up to 2 days or freeze for up to 1 month.

Scallion Oil

Makes about ¾ cup

1 cup vegetable oil

1-inch (2½ cm) piece of fresh ginger, peeled and thinly sliced

1 small onion, sliced

6 scallions, green part only, cut in 1-inch (2½ cm) lengths

1.   Combine all the ingredients in a small saucepan. Set over medium heat and cook, stirring occasionally, until the onion slices turn a rich golden color, 10 to 15 minutes.

2.   Strain, discarding the solids. Let the Scallion Oil cool before using. This can be stored at room temperature for 2 to 3 weeks.

Chile Oil

Makes about 1 cup

1 cup Scallion Oil (see above)

¼ cup pure, red chili powder, preferably Korean

1 cinnamon stick, crushed

1 star anise pod, cracked

1 tablespoon Sichuan peppercorns

1.   Heat the oil in a small saucepan.

2.   In a heatproof bowl, mix the chili powder with 1 tablespoon cold water. Add the cinnamon stick, star anise, and Sichuan peppercorns.

3.   Pour the hot oil over the spice mixture. Let stand overnight, then strain through a fine sieve. Store in a covered jar in the refrigerator for up to 2 weeks.

Chive Oil

Makes about ½ cup

1 bunch chive
⅘ cup vegetable oil
1 teaspoon salt

1.   Put the chives, vegetable oil, and salt in a blender or food processor. Blend for 1 full minute.

2.   Transfer into a bowl set over a larger bowl filled with ice. Chilling will keep the color green. Store in a covered jar in the refrigerator for up to 2 weeks.

Morimoto Special Spice

Makes about ¼ cup

This spicy mixture makes more than you will need for the Lobster Masala recipe on page 94, but keep the remainder to use as a seasoning for any dish that needs perking up.

1 tablespoon chili powder
1 tablespoon sweet paprika
1½ teaspoons salt
¾ teaspoon freshly ground black pepper
¾ teaspoon ground cumin
¾ teaspoon ground coriander
¾ teaspoon ground ginger
¾ teaspoon garam masala
¾ teaspoon cayenne pepper

1.   Combine all of the ingredients.

2.   Store in a covered container in a cool, dark place for up to 3 months.

Five-Spice Powder Morimoto-style

Makes about ⅓ cup

Chinese five-spice powder always includes cinnamon, Sichuan peppercorns, and star anise. The other two spices often vary from brand to brand, but they are usually warm spices like fennel and cloves. I add cumin and coriander to the mix, because I like the slight Indian touch. Traditional Chinese five-spice powder can be purchased in supermarkets, but it will not be as fresh as homemade, and the flavor will be different from mine.

2 tablespoons coriander seeds
2 tablespoons Sichuan peppercorns
2 teaspoons cumin seeds
2 teaspoons ground cinnamon
2 star anise pods

Combine all the ingredients in an electric spice grinder (a coffee grinder dedicated to this purpose) and grind them into a not-too-fine powder or pound in a mortar and pestle. Transfer to a covered container and store in a cool, dark place for up to 3 months.

Sesame Sauce

Makes about ¼ cup

¼ cup sake
3 tablespoons sesame seed
1 tablespoon soy sauce

1.   In a small saucepan, boil the sake over high heat until reduced to 2 tablespoons, 1 to 2 minutes. Let cool completely.

2.   Heat a small dry skillet over medium-high heat. Add the sesame seeds and cook, stirring often, until they are lightly browned and fragrant, about 3 minutes. Transfer the toasted sesame seeds to a dish and let cool.

3.   In a blender or mini processor, grind the sesame seeds well. Add the reduced sake and soy sauce and process to a smooth paste.

Miso Sauce

Both Red and White Miso sauce are used as the bases for many preparations in the book. White miso is softer and sweeter than red miso, so this sauce, also called *saikyo* miso, lends itself to more delicate and light-colored dishes. While the proportions differ slightly, the technique is the same for both.

White Miso Sauce

Makes about 1⅓ cups

1 cup sweet white miso (*saikyo*, available in Asian specialty stores)
2 tablespoons mirin
¼ cup sugar
1 egg yolk

See below for method.

Red Miso Sauce

Makes about 1½ cups

1 cup red miso
3 tablespoons mirin
6 tablespoons sugar
1 egg yolk

1.   In a stainless steel bowl, combine the miso, mirin, sugar, and egg yolk. Whisk together until well combined. Set over a pan of simmering water and whisk constantly until the sugar is

259

dissolved and the mixture is warm, 8 to 10 minutes. Remove from the heat.

2. If not used at once, transfer the Red Miso Sauce to a covered container and refrigerate for up to 5 days (the same goes for the White Miso Sauce).

....

Ponzu Sauce

Makes about 2 cups

This tangy sauce is very popular in Japan. Stored in a covered jar in the refrigerator, the sauce will keep well for up to a month. Note: Since the marinated rinds contribute to the flavor of the sauce, be sure to wash the fruits well before cutting them up.

⅓ lemon

¼ orange

1 cup *ponzu* juice (available in Asian specialty stores)

1 cup soy sauce

⅓ cup sake

6 tablespoons water

6 tablespoons mirin

5 ounces (150 g) bonito flakes

2 sheets of kombu, 4 x 8 inches (10 x 20 cm) each, broken in half

1. Squeeze the juice of the lemon and orange pieces into a large container. Toss in the rinds.

2. Add all the remaining ingredients, cover, and refrigerate for at least a week and up to a month before using.

3. Strain before use.

Yuzu Foam

Makes 3 cups

2 sheets (2 g each) unflavored gelatin

½ cup sugar

½ cup *yuzu* juice, fresh or thawed frozen, or substitute key lime or lime juice

Pinch of salt

1. Dissolve the gelatin in 2 tablespoons of cold water in a small bowl and set aside to soften for about 5 minutes.

2. Put the sugar in a small saucepan. Add ½ cup cold water and bring to a boil, stirring to dissolve the sugar. Remove from the heat.

3. Add the softened gelatin to the sugar and stir until it is completely dissolved. Stir in the *yuzu* juice. Season with the salt. Let cool, then refrigerate until thoroughly chilled, about 2 hours.

4. Pour the *yuzu* mixture into a CO_2 canister and use to garnish plates as desired.

....

Tempura Batter

Makes about 3½ cups

2 large egg yolks

½ cup vegetable oil

1½ cups chilled club soda or seltzer

2 cups tempura flour (available in Asian specialty stores)

1. Beat the egg yolks in a bowl.

2. Whisk in the oil until well blended and then add the club soda.

3. Add the tempura flour and stir with chopsticks just until combined. (Don't worry if some flour floats on top. It is better to under mix rather than over beat.)

Crispy Burdock

Makes about 4 to 6 servings as a garnish

These frizzled strands of the popular Japanese root vegetable turn slightly nutty when fried. They make a great crispy garnish.

1 lemon

1 burdock root, about ½ pound (225 g)

Vegetable oil, for deep frying

1. Fill a medium bowl with cold water and squeeze the lemon juice into the water. With a swivel-bladed vegetable peeler, remove the skin of the burdock. Continue "peeling" the white root to make long strips. As they are peeled, drop them in the acidulated water.

2. In a deep-fat fryer or a large, deep saucepan, heat at last 2 inches (5 cm) of oil to 340°F (170°C).

3. Drain the burdock strips and dry them well. Carefully add to the hot oil in 2 batches—if there is any water remaining on them, it will splatter—and fry until golden brown, about 2 to 3 minutes.

4. Remove the Crispy Burdock with a slotted spoon and drain on paper towels. Season lightly with coarse salt.

Glossary

Asari clams.
Known in the United States as Manila clams, these small, sea-sweet shellfish are not always easy to get. If you can't find them, substitute littlenecks or New Zealand cockles.

Ayu.
Also called sweetfish, this small river fish is often rubbed with salt and grilled. Available frozen in some Asian specialty stores.

Benitade.
Peppery purplish sprouts, also called water pepper. Typically used as a garnish. Available at some Asian specialty stores.

Buri.
Refers to a mature yellowtail, a popular fish more familiar to many diners in its younger form (*hamachi*). Winter is the peak season for yellowtail, when its pale, off-white flesh is lusciously fatty. It can be served as sushi, sashimi, or cooked.

Chunyan.
Sweet rice pudding. Sold in jars in Chinese groceries.

Congee.
This pleasingly porridge-like gruel made from rice and water is popular throughout Asia. Typically served for breakfast, it can be flavored with everything from dried scallops to peanuts.

Daikon.
A large mild, slightly sweet white radish, it is served pickled alongside rice, raw and shredded alongside sashimi, and grated into a fine, moist paste to be mixed into sauces and soups. Available fresh and pickled in Asian specialty stores and some major supermarkets.

Dashi.
A staple Japanese stock typically made from *katsuobushi* (cured and dried *bonito*) and *kombu* (a type of kelp). Unlike French stock, it takes only about 10 minutes to prepare. It is used in everything from soups to stews to sauces. Available powdered in Asian specialty stores, but homemade is nearly as easy to make and has a superior flavor.

Five-spice powder.
A mixture of five or more spices than can include ground cinnamon, cloves, fennel seed, star anise, ginger, and Sichuan peppercorns. It is used in marinades and sauces. Available in most supermarkets. Because of its popularity, even McCormick now makes it.

Fugu.
Blowfish in English, a fish whose poisonous organs are removed prior to serving. It is often served in thin slices of sashimi (*usuzukuri*). Specialty restaurants in Japan create entire meals that consist of blowfish dishes. Only chefs who have gone through rigorous training and obtained a special license can butcher the fish. It is considered a delicacy, and thus is very expensive.

Ginnan.
Ginko nuts are the fall fruits of the gingko tree. Available fresh in their shells as well as canned in Asian specialty stores.

Gobo.
Burdock in English, this long, thin root vegetable is grown primarily in Japan. Available fresh in Asian specialty stores.

Hayashi.
A Japanese-style beef stew with onions and savory stock.

Japanese curry.
Sold in both semisolid and powder form, this ready-to-use spice mixture is used to make Japanese-style curry. Available in Asian specialty stores.

Johakuto.
Japanese sugar in English, this contains inverted sugar. For the recipes in this book, ordinary white cane sugar can be used.

Kabosu.
A citrus fruit with deep-green skin and a tart flavor used to add an acidic note to Japanese sauces and dishes. The juice is available bottled or frozen in some Asian specialty stores. Key lime is the closest substitute.

Kakuni.
Pork belly, which is fresh uncured, unsmoked bacon, braised until it is meltingly tender.

Kampyo.
This sweet sun-dried gourd is commonly simmered in a mixture of soy sauce, sake, and sugar and used as a filling for sushi rolls.

Kare-pan.
Curry pan, or "curry bread" is a snack food found in Japanese bakeries that consists of *panko*-encrusted fried dough that has been filled with curried beef.

Katsuo.
Bonito in English, this member of the mackerel family has rich, dark flesh. It is often served as sashimi and *tataki*, though after it has been cured and dried, it's an essential ingredient for making dashi, the essential Japanese stock.

Kinome.
The young, peppery, fernlike leaves of the prickly ash plant that form in the spring. Typically used as a garnish. Available at some Asian specialty stores.

Kochujan.
A fiery, red paste made from fermented soybeans, red chiles, and glutinous-rice flour, popular in Korea. Available in Asian specialty stores.

Kombu.
Known as kelp in English, this sea vegetable is harvested from Japan's cold waters, mostly near Hokkaido, then dried and used to make dashi stock. It comes in various types and levels of quality. Buy the best you can find from Asian specialty stores.

Konnyaku.
A yam cake made from the same starchy, gelatinous tuber (*konnyaku*) as *shirataki*, this bland, chewy block is cut into large cubes and used in *nimono*, or simmered dishes. Available in Asian specialty stores.

Kukonomi.
Chinese red raisins are also called *goji* berries or wolfberries. These nutritious fruits are eaten dry or soaked and used in sauces. Available in Asian specialty stores.

Kumamoto oysters.
Named for Kumamoto prefecture in Japan, these small oysters are now cultivated on the West Coast of the United States. They have a mildly sweet, lightly briny flavor and a creamy texture.

Lampong.
A black peppercorn grown in Indonesia, that is valued for its flavor and pungency. Available at specialty spice stores and some Asian grocers.

Light-colored soy sauce.
Like the more common dark kind, it is also a sauce made from fermented soybeans and wheat. This version is slightly saltier, lighter in color, and not as thick. Available at Asian specialty stores and some supermarkets.

Longan.
A grape-size fruit with brown skin and sweet, translucent flesh. Available in Asian specialty stores.

Lotus leaf.
The large leaves of the lotus, a water plant, is sold dried. The fan-shaped, green-brown leaves are often used as wrappers for ingredients that are then steamed or grilled. They impart a pleasantly musky, earthy flavor. Available at Asian specialty stores.

Matsutake.
Literally "pine mushroom" in English, these fungi grow beneath pine trees in the fall. Served simply grilled, or steamed in a pot with broth, they are prized for their woodsy aroma and can be very expensive.

Menegi.
These tender, thin young chives have a subtle peppery flavor, much like wild chives. Available fresh in some Asian specialty stores.

Mirin.
Fortified wine made from glutinous rice and used solely for cooking. Available in most Asian specialty stores.

Miso.
Fermented soybean paste that comes in three basic varieties: miso made just from soybeans (*mamemiso*), miso made from

barley and soybeans (*mugimiso*), and miso made from rice and soybeans (*komemiso*); the latter is the most common. *Akamiso*, also called red or brown miso, refers to a salty type of *mugimiso* or *komemiso* that has been fermented for about a year. *Shiromiso*, or white miso, is fermented for much less time and tastes much sweeter. An especially sweet type of *shiromiso* called *saikyo miso* is made in Kyoto, Japan. Most of these varieties are available at Asian specialty stores and some health food stores.

Mitsuba.
An herb that resembles cilantro in appearance, and a combination of parsley, celery, and chervil in taste, it is often used as a garnish and in soups. Available fresh in Asian specialty stores.

Mizuame.
A sweet clear jelly made from millet. Sold in Japanese specialty stores. Light corn syrup can be used as a substitute.

Monkfish liver.
Ankimo in Japanese, monkfish liver is typically steamed and served with *ponzu* sauce and scallions. It tastes rich, with a whiff of both foie gras and the sea. Available from some seafood purveyors.

Natsume.
Also called jujubes, Chinese dates are brown, olive-size, slightly sweet fruit, sold fresh and dried in Asian specialty stores.

Nori.
An aquatic plant that's harvested, minced to a paste, formed into paperlike sheets, and dried. Most Americans are familiar with nori as the blackish green wrapper for

sushi rolls. It is also used in soups and shredded and served atop rice. Quality and price varies widely. Available in Asian specialty stores.

Obrato.
An edible transparent sheet made from water mixed with either rice flour or the pith of the stems from the rice-paper plant.

Omakase.
Roughly translated as "chef's choice," this refers to a meal typically composed of small dishes chosen by the chef.

Panko.
Coarse bread crumbs favored in Japan to coat fried foods because they remain crisp even as they cool. Available in most Asian specialty stores and some supermarkets.

Ponzu.
A tart dipping sauce typically made from rice vinegar, soy sauce, dashi, and citrus juice (*yuzu* or *sudachi*). Its bright flavor enlivens sashimi and grilled meats. Although bottled versions are available in Asian specialty stores, it pays to make your own.

Red bean paste.
An in Japanese, this is made from sugar and *azuki* beans and used as a filling for confections. Available in Asian specialty stores.

Sake.
Often misleadingly called "rice wine," this alcoholic beverage is brewed from water and rice by a process similar to beer making. While wine is categorized according to the grapes with which it is made, sake is classified by the degree to which the rice used is polished. *Junmai*

refers to sake made from rice that has been polished until about 70% of each grain remains; *ginjo* refers to sake made from rice polished until no more than 60% of each grain remains; and *dai ginjo* refers to that made from rice polished until about 50% of each grain remains. Available at shops devoted to sake and at many wine shops and Asian specialty stores.

Sansho pepper.
The seedpod of the prickly ash tree, it is usually served ground, dusted on top of finished foods to add its unique flavor, or as part of the seven-spice blend called *shichimi togarashi*, which is used to spice everything from *yakitori* (grilled chicken skewers) to grilled eel.

Shirataki.
Long thin, transparent noodles made from the starchy, gelatinous tuber called *konnyaku*. They are either boiled or dry-roasted in a pan before using to make stir-fries, soups, and even desserts. Available fresh and canned in Asian specialty stores.

Shiso.
From the *perilla* or beefsteak plant, this highly aromatic jagged-edge green leaf tastes like a cross between mint and basil. It is most often used raw to perfume everything from salads to sushi rolls. Available fresh at Asian specialty stores.

Shisonomi.
Leaf buds of the *shiso* plant, this hard-to-find ingredient is used as a garnish and occasionally sold fresh in Asian specialty stores.

Sichuan peppercorn.
Not actually a peppercorn, but the husk of the seed from a plant

that's a member of the citrus family. Used often in China's Sichuan province, it is famous for producing a pleasant numbing, burning sensation. Available in Asian specialty stores and specialty spice shops.

Soy sauce.
There are a number of different soy sauces used for different effects in Japanese cooking. The most common soy sauce is ordinary *shoyu*, a soy sauce made from fermented soybeans and wheat. (Not to be confused with light-colored soy sauce or white soy sauce, both of which I use in some recipes; see Soy Sauce on page 136). *Shoyu* varies widely in quality, from the mass-produced type to artisanal sauces that are aged for more than 30 years.

Sudachi.
Closely related to the *yuzu*, this small citrus fruit is used when it's green and unripe for its zest and tart juice. Available fresh at some Asian specialty stores, though as with *yuzu* and *kabosu*, it is easier to find the fruit's juice bottled or frozen. Key lime would be the closest substitute.

Sweet rice.
Also called glutinous rice, this is steamed, pounded into a paste, and used to make *mochi*, a sticky rice cake. Available in Asian specialty stores.

Surimi.
A paste made from ground seafood, often formed into cakes or used in place of crab in California rolls. Available in Asian specialty stores.

Takenoko.
The young, tender shoots of the bamboo tree. They are available

fresh in some Asian specialty stores. Canned bamboo shoots can be substituted, though the flavor will not be the same.

Takoyaki.
A popular Osaka street snack often eaten with a toothpick, it comprises octopus-filled balls of batter topped with a thick, tangy sauce and flakes of dried bonito.

Tamari.
A slightly darker and thicker soy sauce made without wheat. Available in most supermarkets.

Tobanjan.
Chinese chile-bean paste. Available in Asian specialty stores.

Tonkatsu sauce.
A slightly sweet, tangy Worcestershire-based sauce typically served with fried, breaded pork cutlet. Available in Asian specialty stores and many supersmarkets.

Tofuyo.
Pungent fermented tofu, from Okinawa. Crumbled feta cheese would be the best substitute for this hard-to-find delicacy.

Udon noodles.
Thick, white noodles made from a mixture of water and wheat flour. *Inaniwa udon* are a thinner variety, used in some dishes. Sold fresh and dried, they are available in Asian specialty stores.

Uni.
Often called sea urchin, *uni* is actually what you find when you crack one open—both the roe and the sweet, briny custardlike gonads. It is most often served raw as sushi and sashimi. Available fresh, even occasionally

live, at specialty seafood purveyors and by mail order.

Usuzukuri.
A method of cutting firm-fleshed fish, such as fluke and *fugu*, into very thin slices. Often served with *ponzu* sauce for dipping.

Wagyu.
Literally "Japanese cattle," this term refers to the beef imported from Japan. In America, Wagyu cattle are crossbred with domestic cattle and sold as "domestic Wagyu." Both the Japanese and U.S. varieties are often sold as "Kobe beef," but genuine Kobe beef is only raised in the Kobe region of Japan. Available at specialty butcher shops.

Wasabi.
A wild plant that grows in shallows streams in the mountains of Japan and is now cultivated in the United States. The knobby green rhizome has a horseradishlike bite. It is often ground to a paste and served with sushi and sashimi. Wasabi leaves are sometimes pickled or fried as tempura. Though it is best when grated from the fresh rhizome, it is often sold as a premade paste. High-quality pastes are available, but many substitute mustard powder for real wasabi. It is available fresh in some Asian specialty stores; wasabi paste is available in many major supermarkets.

Yamanoimo.
Japanese mountain potato in English, this yam is often grated, which produces a slightly gooey texture. It is sometimes used as a dip for raw tuna. Available in Asian specialty stores.

Yamamomo.
Literally "mountain peach," a sweet-tart red fruit, sometimes died dark green, the size of a large olive. Used as a garnish, in desserts, and to make liquor. Available fresh in some Asian specialty stores.

Yukari.
This sour powder is made from Japanese red shiso leaves and is available at some Asian specialty stores.

Yuzu.
A small, tart citrus fruit that tastes like a cross between a lemon, a lime, and an orange. It is used both for its zest and its juice. Some Asian specialty stores carry the fresh fruit, but you'll more commonly find its juice in bottles or frozen and its rind dried. Substitute lemon in a pinch.

Zenmai.
The immature, tightly curled tips of the royal fern. Available jarred at some Asian specialty stores. Fiddlehead ferns make a fine substitute.

Sources

Asian Food Grocer
131 West Harris Avenue
South San Francisco, CA 94080
(888) 482-2742
www.asianfoodgrocer.com

The online arm of a veteran wholesaler, this site is a great source for Japanese ingredients such as *shirataki* noodles, frozen eel, ten types of miso, and wasabi paste. Ships nationwide.

Catalina Offshore Products
5202 Lovelock Street
San Diego, CA 92110
(619) 297-9797
www.catalinaop.com

Based in San Diego, Catalina Offshore Products is an amazing source of fresh and frozen sushi-grade fish and seafood such as yellowtail, whole red snapper, and exceptional sea urchin harvested off the coast from Santa Barbara. Ships nationwide.

Kalustyan's
123 Lexington Avenue
New York, NY 10016
(800) 352-3451
www.Kalustyans.com

This extraordinary New York spice shop may focus on Indian ingredients, but its extensive roster also includes Chinese five-spice powder, *shichimi togarashi*, many different varieties of rice, bonito flakes, and seaweed. Ships nationwide.

Korin
57 Warren Street
New York, NY 10007
(800) 626-2172
www.korin.com

This venerable knife shop in New York sells and ships its fine kitchen equipment and tableware. Along with knives, plates, and bento boxes, it offers hard-to-find items like *bincho tan* charcoal, sharkskin wasabi graters, and bonito shavers. Ships nationwide.

Lobel's of New York
1096 Madison Avenue
New York, NY 10028
(877) 783-4512
www.lobels.com

One of American's most respected butcher shops, Lobel's ships its exceptional (and expensive) meats anywhere in the U.S. Along with lamb, sausages, and dry-aged porterhouse steaks, the shop sells American Wagyu beef and high-fat (and more important high-flavor) Kurobuta pork.

Maruwa, Inc.
10562 San Pablo Avenue
El Cerrito, CA 94530
(510) 528-5210
www.maruwa.com

While their Web site is a little confusing, this Japanese market mini-chain in the San Francisco Bay area delivers nationwide such essential Japanese pantry items as *udon* and *soba* noodles, sweet rice, pickled plums, and *sansho* powder.

Mitsuwa Marketplace
595 River Road
Edgewater, NJ 07020
(201) 941-9113

333 South Alameda Street
Los Angeles, CA 90013
(213) 687-6699
www.mitsuwa.com

This supermarket chain has one of the biggest selections of Japanese food outside of Japan. While their Web site is not yet set up for shopping, it does give their other seven locations across the nation.

Uwajimaya
600 5th Avenue South
Seattle, WA 98104
(206) 624-6248
www.uwajimaya.com

One of the largest Asian grocery retailers in the Pacific Northwest, Uwajimaya also has locations in Bellevue and Beaverton, Washington. The Web site includes recipes and ingredient descriptions—and a link to purchase from www.amazon.com.

Index

Acknowledgments

I would like to thank all of my chefs at my restaurants in New York, Philadelphia, Mumbai, and Tokyo, without whose dedication and support I would not have been able to succeed in my restaurant ventures and this book. In particular, I'd like to thank chefs Makoto Okuwa, Manabu Inoue, Takao Iinuma, Yoshinori Ishii, Hisanobu Osaka, Fumihiko Sakaguchi, Ariki Omae, and Takeshi Omae, who provided special support in testing and finalizing recipes, and assisting in preparation.

I'd also like to thank Susan Wyler for helping to shape the recipes and the scope of the book; JJ Goode for his work on the features and writing the introduction and glossary, Marilyn Anthony for her help in home recipe-testing. I'd like to thank the whole team at DK Publishing, especially my editor, Anja Schmidt, as well as Kim Witherspoon and Eleanor Jackson at Inkwell Management. Special thanks to my personal assistant, Chiaki Takada, and to Mark Stone.